MOON, MAGIC, MIXOLOGY

From *Lunar Love Spell Sangria* to the *Solar Eclipse Sour*,
70 Celestial Drinks Infused with Cosmic Power

JULIA HALINA HADAS
Author of *WitchCraft Cocktails*

ADAMS MEDIA
NEW YORK LONDON TORONTO SYDNEY NEW DELHI

Adams Media
An Imprint of Simon & Schuster, Inc.
100 Technology Center Drive
Stoughton, Massachusetts 02072

First Adams Media hardcover edition November 2021

ADAMS MEDIA and colophon are trademarks of Simon & Schuster.

For information about special discounts for bulk purchases, please contact Simon & Schuster Special Sales at 1-866-506-1949 or business@simonandschuster.com.

The Simon & Schuster Speakers Bureau can bring authors to your live event. For more information or to book an event contact the Simon & Schuster Speakers Bureau at 1-866-248-3049 or visit our website at www.simonspeakers.com.

Interior design by Sylvia McArdle
Photographs by Harper Point Photography
Illustrations by Emma Taylor

Manufactured in the United States of America

10 9 8 7 6 5 4 3 2 1

Library of Congress Cataloging-in-Publication Data
Names: Hadas, Julia Halina, author.
Title: Moon, magic, mixology / Julia Halina Hadas.
Description: First Adams Media hardcover edition. | Stoughton, Massachusetts: Adams Media, an imprint of Simon & Schuster, Inc., 2021. | Includes bibliographical references and index.
Identifiers: LCCN 2021021465 | ISBN 9781507216644 (hc) | ISBN 9781507216651 (ebook)
Subjects: LCSH: Alcoholic beverages. | Moon--Miscellanea. | Magic. | LCGFT: Cookbooks.
Classification: LCC TP505 .H27 2021 | DDC 641.2/1--dc23
LC record available at https://lccn.loc.gov/2021021465

ISBN 978-1-5072-1664-4
ISBN 978-1-5072-1665-1 (ebook)

DEDICATION

To Charlotte and Laura,
for putting me on this path.

CONTENTS

SPRING LUNAR LIBATIONS   164

SUMMER
LUNAR LIBATIONS   191

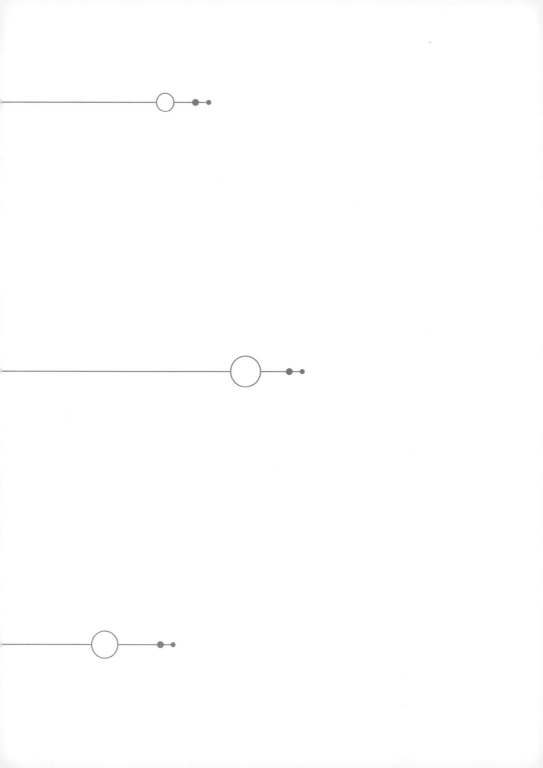

ACKNOWLEDGMENTS

A book is the manifestation of the support, labor, and energy of so many different people. To my family, friends, and peers: I am thankful for your endless support, especially to my mother, Rolf, Nicole, and Rowan. And to everyone at Adams Media: Thank you so much for your hard work in bringing this book to fruition! Special thanks to Eileen, Sarah, Sylvia, and Mary Kate for your continuous guidance, wisdom, and patience.

To all my readers: Connecting with all of you has uplifted me in countless ways that I cannot adequately express. Know that you have all meant so much to me! And to the works that have come before me, enabling me to stand on your shoulders and even attempt to craft this book in the first place, I am forever grateful.

To try and capture the moon in a glass is an almost impossible task, and I'm sure I could've done it many other ways. The moon is an endless source of inspiration for transformation, reflection, and magic that illuminates my every waking moment. I am forever grateful for its wisdom, and I hope I can share that here with you!

I also want to give thanks and acknowledge that I live on Muwekma Ohlone Land.

INTRODUCTION

Since the beginning of time, the moon has been at the heart of many mystical practices, inspiring the rituals, spells, and celebrations carried out on a given night, month, or season. The spring pink moon may enhance spells surrounding new beginnings or love, while the moon passing through the Leo constellation encourages creativity and self-expression. And, as one who practices cosmic crafts knows, full moons are perfect for energy amplification.

In *Moon, Magic, Mixology*, such lunar magic workings are given a delicious new edge. In Part 1, you will learn how the power of the moon can extend beyond basic rituals or celebrations into potent astral potions that can heighten or even serve as complete energy workings, manifestation magic, spells, and more. Organized by season, the recipes in Part 2 draw on the forces of the moons and moon phases that occur in fall, winter, spring, and summer.

Celebrate the abundance of a harvest moon with a spicy Harvest Moon Michelada, channel artistic inspiration under the Pisces moon with a golden Pisces Moon Chai Latte, and embrace the power of transformation through the color-changing Lunar Alchemy.

You'll also delve deeper into the special connection between lunar ritual and alcohol, and how various herbal ingredients, liqueurs, and more can be deliberately blended to call on the magic of the cosmos. While it is tempting to rush ahead, look through these initial pages before crafting your own concoctions so that you can unleash the true lunar potential of the recipes.

Whether you're looking for a perfect beverage to share at your moon circle, a charmed brew to call down the power of the moon during your favorite rituals, or a delicious libation to celebrate the cosmos at any time of year, there's a celestial potion for every occasion.

PART 1

THE WORLD OF MOON MAGIC & MIXOLOGY

Thousands of years ago, crops for alcohol production were sown and harvested in sync with the moon. In modern day, seasoned "selenophiles" and beginning moon worshippers alike craft moon water and tinctures under the full moon. While the moon and alcohol may seem very separate, their history paints another story. In the following chapters, you will learn more about the connection between the moon and alcohol. You'll also uncover the best ways to utilize each moon phase and occasional moon in magic workings, as well as the bartending tools, techniques, and ingredients you'll need to stir up the drinks in Part 2.

CHAPTER 1

ALCOHOL & THE MOON INTERTWINED

To many societies through history, the moon was (and still is) a key marker of time and the passage of the seasons, and an important source of luminescence during the darker months of the year. But the worship of the moon extends far beyond practical value, with its significance and power plunging deep into the spiritual roots of many ancient cultures. A powerful entity of abundance, agriculture, water, and even the afterlife, the moon has been invoked for healing, transformation, and wisdom in countless traditions. More surprising, however, is its ties to the beginnings of alcohol.

In this chapter you will trace the mystical connections of the moon and alcohol in spells, rituals, and celebrations of the past and present, and how this relationship can be enhanced through magical cocktails. It's time for your journey into celestial mixology to begin.

ANCIENT MAGIC, THE MOON, AND ALCOHOL

Sometimes referred to as "water of life," alcohol was seen by a number of ancient cultures as an extension of the bodies of water that the moon manipulated with its phases. The moon was also used as a guide for agriculture, indicating when to sow, trim, and harvest various plants such as grains, grapes, and other ingredients used to craft alcohol. Thus, alcohols like beer and wine were an important part of the celebrations for various harvest cycles and full moons.

In fact, as far back as the earliest known civilization of Sumer, the enchanted relationship between the moon and alcohol can be found within ritual, celebration, and spellcraft. In Sumer, the act of drinking beer was so sacred, it was carved on a lapis lazuli seal on the tomb of Queen Pu-abi, a priestess of the moon god Nanna, or Sin. In an ancient writing, Nanna was given credit for the creation of beer, although this was likely a metaphor to depict Nanna's importance and power, since the creation or embodiment of beer was designated to the goddess Ninkasi. However, given the moon's impact on the harvest that produced the very grains from which beer was—and still is—made, such a metaphor wasn't far from reality.

In Chinese lore, a woman named Chang'e drank an elixir of life and floated up to the moon, becoming a moon goddess. Missing her, Chang'e's husband, Hou Yi, would leave her favorite desserts out every night, a practice that continues today through lunar offerings at the annual Mid-Autumn Festival celebrated in many East and Southeast Asian regions. (Not to mention the importance of the lunar new year to these cultures.)

This connection between the moon and a perceived elixir or beverage of immortality can also be seen in ancient Hinduism. In Hindu mythology, a fermented juice called soma, thought of as an elixir of immortality, was consumed by both the priests and gods and was believed to promote healing and prosperity. Over time, soma was so important it actually became its own deity. Made from herbs that are speculated to include hallucinogenic mushrooms, pomegranate, blue lotus, and either milk or sap from the *Asclepias acida* plant, it seems only natural that soma also became associated with the moon god Chandra. As lord of herbs and the moon, Chandra's lunar harvest was crucial to the ingredients that made this sacred alcohol.

MAGICAL SHIFTS

Much like the moon's own changing shape and repeating cycles, the importance and meaning of the moon has waxed and waned through the years before its modern revival. For example, while some earlier ancient hunter-gatherer societies associated the moon with male and female deities, the moon became more and more associated with feminine gods after the Agricultural Revolution. Some societies, such as the ancient Greeks and Romans, even had a different goddess associated with different aspects of the moon. Selene, for example, was sometimes viewed as the moon personified, while Hecate, as an intermediary of the worlds, was worshipped with the dark moon. And Artemis was seen as ruling over the moon. For other cultures, the moon shifted from a celestial deity who ruled the ocean tides and the night sky to a timekeeper by whom the days of religious events were determined. Perhaps due to the moon's bewitching power, the moon also later became associated with witches dancing underneath the full moon.

But some things remained constant. To medieval astrologers, the moon symbolized the spirit, the soul, and the innermost sanctum of one's unconscious mind and self—a symbolism many astrologers still believe in today. And the moon has remained a close guide for farming practices for cultures across the globe.

With the invention of the printing press in the 1400s, the moon took center stage in literature and shined through in romantic poetry. Words like *lunacy* and *moonstruck* marked the moon's prevalence over emotional states and even love. In fact, the word *moonshine* eventually became associated with alcohol because moonshiners were making money through illegal alcohol operations during the dark of night through the Prohibition era—giving a new meaning to making alcohol under the moon.

MIXING UP THE MOON TODAY

Whether laying out a bowl of water to charge under the moonlight or meditating in congruence with the lunar cycles, it's easy to see the moon is still very much a part of spellcraft and spirituality today. When it comes to liquid magic in particular, the modern moon worshipper often celebrates the moon and utilizes its power with moon water. You can craft moon water by placing a jar of water outside under the moonlight, with the intent that the water will capture or be "charged" by the energetic vibration of that moon phase. It's often drunk, added to bathwater, turned into magical moon mists, or used for scrying. A spellcrafter will often use alcohol to preserve moon water over a longer period of time for magical purposes.

You can also charge alcohol under moonlight, or chill an alcoholic drink with ice cubes made from magical moon water (more on this in Chapter 4). And just like many ancient cultures did, some modern wineries harvest grapes for their products in sync with the moon.

Today, wine and other mixed beverages are often brought to imbibe at moon harvest celebrations and other lunar rituals. In some Wiccan practices, ritual participants may drink from a chalice of alcohol, before leaving the remainder as an offering to various deities, some of which are directly associated with the moon. Slowly but surely, the power and potential of mixology is sweeping its way through the world of magic with deliciously aligned elixirs.

Elevating the Relationship

The mystical connection between the moon and drink can be traced through time and practice. But there is so much more that can be done with this relationship—so much more potential to unlock! The countless edible herbs and other flavors used in today's craft beverage industry have resonating correspondences in magic workings involving the moon. For example, cucumber and rose can be used to enhance beauty with the moon in Cancer or Libra. And grapefruit and rosemary can elevate a lunar purification spell during the banishing waning moon. By blending these enchanted elements in alcohol, you create a drinkable potion that can enhance a ritual, spell, celebration, or other lunar endeavor. A cocktail can even act as a complete spell!

The very act of gathering, mixing, and pouring the ingredients to create your cocktail can itself be a part of the magic, providing space for you to focus your energy on what you are hoping to manifest with the moon through the drink. After all, an important part of any bewitched work is visualization—imagining what it would look and feel like to achieve your goal. For example, perhaps you are hoping to take advantage of the vibrant Leo moon to feel more confident and become the life of the party. If you don't tune in to what that confidence would look and feel like, it may be difficult to truly believe in that outcome. And if you don't believe in it, it is far less likely to come true, no matter the enchantment you cast. Sipping an aligned cocktail beforehand can help inspire the energy you seek, and promote confidence in the magical work ahead.

As you continue through the following chapters, you will uncover more and more of the mystical powers found in combining witchcraft with alcohol.

ETHICS AND RESPONSIBILITY

Lunar infusions are a wonderful way to manifest magic in every aspect of your life; however, as a steward of all the moon holds sacred, it's important that you practice moon mixology ethically. It is best to source ingredients through sustainable, ethical, and culturally cognizant methods as much as possible. This can mean buying herbs that are fair trade, organic, and sustainably harvested from local farmers, harvest shops, or online independent sellers. It also means taking care to respect different traditions and cultures as you source your ingredients. Additionally, you can buy crystals for energetically enjoying alongside your magical beverages directly from ethical sources or independent miners (just be sure to never put them in your drink unless you are confident they are nontoxic!). Be sure to read up on any safety and proper use instructions from legitimate sources before you use any herbs or unfamiliar ingredients in your creations. Consider asking your doctor for their recommendations as well.

Additionally, be sure to always drink responsibly. As the ancient Sumerians understood, alcohol's sacred associations mean it should be treated as such, with rules and boundaries around its enjoyment. Everything in moderation is always a good rule. Keep in mind that all libations under the moon are magical—alcoholic or not. You can turn many cocktails into nonalcoholic beverages with easy swaps. A general rule of thumb is to replace the alcohol with soda water and vary the citrus-to-sugar ratios accordingly to taste. Liqueur flavors can sometimes be replaced by fresh ingredients, juices, or syrups.

READYING FOR DELICIOUS MOON MAGIC

Now that you have a clearer understanding of how the moon and alcohol are intertwined, you're ready to explore the mixology tools, tricks, and ingredients for making every beverage under the sun—or in this case, the moon! There is so much more to enchanted drinks than a glass and tasty flavors, so you won't want to skip this information. Read on to delve deeper into the magic of lunar cocktails.

CHAPTER 2

MIXOLOGY
OF THE MOON

As the radiance of the full moon extends out to touch her window, a woman places a jar of water on the windowsill to charge in the mystical moonlight. Another selenophile places his favorite crystals outside his door to cleanse in the lunar rays. Many modern moon worshippers carefully select crystals, candles, and herbs to attune their meditations, healing, and intentions to a particular moon. Why not do the same with tasty drinks? With moon mixology, you can align potent beverages to the various moons and moon themes.

In this chapter, you will uncover the energetic potential of various alcoholic spirits, as well as the basics of mixology and the magical associations of popular cocktail flavors. Everything you need to stir up martinis, tropical drinks, adult coffees, and more like a pro mixologist is here. It's time to roll out the cosmic bar cart!

LUNAR SPIRITS

While ancient cultures tied the moon to the oldest alcoholic libations of wine and beer, a plethora of other ingredients are available today thanks to the modern craft beverage movement. From beer and wine cultivated over thousands of years to relatively modern distilled spirits like vodka, gin, and tequila, there is a myriad of elements you can stir into your lunar chalice. In the following sections, you will learn about each of the spirits that are used to infuse the magical concoctions in Part 2.

Beer

From the recipes recorded by the ancient Sumerians to those crafted by modern breweries, beer is steeped in history. Dating possibly as far back as 10,000 B.C.E., beer is one of the oldest alcoholic beverages that civilization still enjoys today. It is created by brewing and fermenting grains such as wheat, barley, rye, corn, and rice, which have a potent starch content. The two most common beer categories are lagers and ales.

In magical mixology, beer is a great choice for celebrating the harvest moons and connecting to ancient wisdom, due to its cereal grain base. It is also associated with purification—in fact, beer spas have recently begun popping up throughout Europe, and some are now emerging in the US. Beer can be drunk as is, or poured over a cocktail for a unique celebratory beverage.

Sake

Sake is made from the fermentation of rice. Native to Japan and parts of China, it is created following a similar process to beer. Sake-specific rice is polished, steamed to promote the conversion of starch to sugar, and then mixed with water and yeast to ferment and convert the sugars to alcohol. Some sake brew masters specifically grow the koji spore for sake fermentation. This spore can grow for 18–35 days before the sake is then pressed, filtered, pasteurized, and sometimes aged for up to six months.

As it is made from rice, sake can be added to lunar concoctions to manifest abundance, luck, protection, sensuality, and creativity.

Wine

Wine, like beer, is one of the oldest alcohols intentionally created and has occupied an important role across cultures throughout human history. Typically, wine is made from the fermented juice of grapes, but it is occasionally made from other fermented fruits. Various ancient cultures independently developed their own varieties of wine, and the ancient Egyptians may have been the first to document the process of wine making. In wine making, everything from the climate to the soil in which the grapes grow plays a huge part in the flavor produced. Today, there are biodynamic wine makers who actually practice wine making in sync with the moon!

The color of wine is determined by whether or not the skins of red grapes are allowed to ferment along with the juice. In white wine, the skins are removed in the earlier stages of the fermentation process. In red wine, the skins are left on throughout the process, and in rosé, they are removed partway through fermentation. Thus, a red grape can be made into a white wine, but a white grape cannot be made into a red wine.

With skins left on, red wine is associated with the physical body, vitality, sensuality, energy, and ancestors. As the skins are removed to create white wine, the energy of the wine is more spiritual and soul-aligned. Rosé, with its pink hue, is often associated with love, and as the in-between of red and white wine, can represent a connection between the physical and spiritual. Because it is made from grapes, wine can generally be used in magical mixology to manifest money and fertility, and to enhance the mind and one's dreams.

Sparkling Wine

Sparkling wines are wines that contain carbon dioxide. Two such wines are prosecco, a dry wine from Italy, and champagne, which is made from a combination of grapes grown in the Champagne region of France. As a carbonated variation, sparkling wine shares the energetic associations of white wine. However, it is often used for celebrations as well, and with its bubbles, it can be especially associated with spirit.

Vermouth

From the traditional martini to the Americano, vermouth plays a central role in craft cocktails. While the definition of vermouth can vary based on country, vermouths are generally aromatic wines fortified with herbs and spices. As is the case with various proprietary liqueurs, some vermouth recipes are secret. Most types of vermouth are designated as either sweet or dry. Often called red vermouth, sweet vermouth was once made from red wine but is now also made from white wine. Essential for classics like the Manhattan, sweet vermouth uses various sweetened herbs and spices for a richer flavor. In contrast, dry vermouth has no sugar added and is traditionally made from white wine. The lack of sugar expresses more dryness on the tongue, and these vermouths tend to have a more citrusy taste.

As a fortified wine, vermouth can be used for similar magical purposes to wine. However, with various herbal infusions, vermouths also carry enhanced energetic vibrations that depend on the specific ingredients used.

Brandy

While there is some debate over what constitutes a brandy, they are generally made from distilled wine. They should not be confused with fruit brandies, which are often infused with fruits and sweetened. Cognac, pisco, and Armagnac fall into the brandy category. Some brandies are aged in wooden barrels, others are color-enhanced, and some are both barrel-aged and color-enhanced. These processes give brandy a dark appearance.

Depending on whether it is aged in barrels made of wood, such as oak, brandy can carry additional magical properties of protection, strength, and wisdom. Originating from grapes, brandy carries on the magic and potency of this fruit's spirit.

Vodka

From the signature screwdriver to the cosmopolitan, the world of mixology would not be the same without vodka. Likely originating in either Poland or Russia, vodka is typically defined as a neutral distilled spirit. While many think vodka is made solely from potatoes or wheat, it can actually be made from any fermentable substance if brought to a high enough proof. While vodka is considered a "neutral" distilled spirit, varying vodkas can possess significant flavor differences as well as highlight subtle elements based on the substances they are made from, the stills used in creation, how they are filtered, and how much water is added (and from what water sources). While it took the creation of the Moscow Mule to spread the gospel of vodka in the United States, it is now 31 percent of the US spirits market—and most of the market in Eastern Europe. Vodka is popular beyond its use in drinking, for crafting herbal tinctures, preserving energetically charged waters, and creating mists. (Everclear, while not a vodka, is similarly defined as a neutral grain spirit, brought to such a high proof that it is often used to craft bitters.)

In lunar mixology, the magic of your vodka may depend on the root of its creations (potato, grain, different fruits, etc.). Due to its neutrality and clarity, it is a great choice for a variety of magical intentions, especially for clarity, cleansing, protection, and connecting to spiritual forces.

Gin

While vodka can be made from a number of organic substances, gin is defined solely by the addition and prominent flavor of juniper berries. At whatever point the juniper is added as an infusion, either after or before distillation, the beverage becomes gin. Oftentimes, distilleries will add various other herbal flavors to complement and bring out the unique flavors of this otherwise herbal, medicinal beverage.

Juniper's protective, purifying associations make gin a go-to for cleansing, reversing, psychic, and protective cocktails.

Tequila and Mezcal

Made from agave, tequila and mezcal embody the magic of this amazing plant. Taking 10–25 years to bloom, the plant must be quickly harvested right as it blooms to capture its sugars before it dies soon after flowering. Its unique life cycle offers a reflection on life and death cycles, as well as coming to one's power. Tequila is made solely from the blue agave plant and is primarily produced in the state of Jalisco in Mexico. Mezcal can be made from any kind of agave plant. Unless labeled "blanco" or "silver," tequila is aged in wood barrels that allow for a more complex flavor. The amount of time the spirit has been aged leads to the designation of blanco/silver, reposado, and anejo tequila.

Agave has magical associations with love and lust but is also tied to worship in Central and South America. Due to its unique life cycle, agave can also be associated with rejuvenation and used for magical workings around stepping into one's power.

Whiskey

Whiskey (also spelled *whisky* depending on the country of origin) is made from a mash of fermented grains, such as barley, corn, rye, or wheat. Different types of whiskeys, such as Irish, Scotch, Japanese, Canadian, and Tennessee, all have varying legal qualifications that they must fulfill in order to be sold under this naming umbrella, from base grains used to the type of barrel the drink is aged in, or even how it is filtered. Depending on the percentage of the grain mixture, this can give way to bourbon (made from at least 51 percent corn mash and produced in the United States) or rye (made from at least 51 percent rye) whiskeys. After distillation, the alcohol is then aged in barrels (often charred oak barrels), where the alcohol soaks up nuanced flavors over time.

With the influence of grains and oak, whiskey is another prominent alcohol for the harvest season, as well as for grounding, ancestral work, and prosperity. Since the grains that make whiskey hold the promise of the future, as well as the energy of the past, whiskey can also be great for reflection on life cycles.

Rum

Rum is distilled from either the molasses, syrup, or fermented juice of sugarcane. While sugarcane was enjoyed for years prior, distillation of sugarcane to create rum didn't occur until the seventeenth century on Caribbean sugarcane plantations. These plantations used slaves to grow, maintain, and harvest this plant, and thus it is important to recognize rum's connection to slavery. From this time, many Afro-Caribbean diaspora traditions began integrating the rum they crafted into their spiritual practices. Once distillation began, rum quickly became popular. Generally, light or white rums are filtered after any barrel aging to remove color. Comparatively, dark rums may have extensive aging and heavier body, be colored with burnt sugar or caramel, and even be infused with various fruits and spices.

Stemming from sugarcane, rum can be great for workings around love, lust, abundance, and a sweet disposition. It can also be used as a lunar offering.

Absinthe

Once infamously known as the "green fairy" and believed to cause hallucinations (though modern research has found that this effect was likely widely overstated and not caused by the alcohol itself), absinthe is flavored with anise, wormwood, and other herbal ingredients like fennel that give it a licorice-like taste. Absinthe is a must-have for classic drinks like Death in the Afternoon and the Sazerac.

With the protective, psychic, and spirit-conjuring associations of wormwood and anise, absinthe is a great choice for calling down the moon to aid in psychic abilities, purification, and communicating with spirits, as well as for making love and protection enchantments. And as writer Ernest Hemingway knew, it is also a choice spirit for creative inspiration!

Liqueurs

Mixtures of alcohol, sugar, and flavoring agents such as flowers, herbs, and fruits are used to create the liqueurs essential for a number of delicious and classic cocktails. The White Russian would not be possible without coffee liqueur, and the Godfather can't be made without amaretto, an almond-flavored liqueur. In the US, the word *cordial* is often used to refer to some liqueurs, but this word is also used for nonalcoholic fruit beverages in other countries.

Liqueurs, like most ingredients used in mixology, started off as a way to preserve herbal remedies for medicinal purposes. In some circumstances, this resulted in proprietary recipes, like Green Chartreuse, made by a group of monks in the French Alps since 1840. Today, a distinct group of liqueurs called amari (singular: amaro), bitter herbal Italian liqueurs originally crafted with plant-based medicinal agents to stimulate appetite and digestion, are responsible for a variety of beloved beverages, such as Aperol for the Aperol Spritz or Campari for the classic Negroni. Some liqueurs used in Part 2 are amaretto, anise liqueur (also called anisette), crème de cacao, and triple sec. Some liqueurs are relatively easy to make; recipes for these are included in Chapter 4. Others are more complicated, so it's best to buy them premade.

To match a liqueur up properly for aligned lunar magic, check the magical associations of the main flavoring ingredient in the Edible Elements section in Chapter 3 of this book. The magic of a liqueur will depend on what it is made out of.

Bitters

Similar to liqueurs, bitters started off as a tonic to quell maladies and preserve herbal remedies, and thus several proprietary blends have been crafted through the years. In essence, bitters are highly concentrated elixirs typically (though not always) composed of high-proof alcohol and flavoring agents like roots, flowers, bark, and other botanicals, the combination of which results in a strong, bitter liquid. Often just a few drops can transform and bring together a concoction. The most popular brand of bitters is Angostura. You will learn how to make your own bitters for lunar cocktails in Chapter 4, but you can also buy premade versions.

You can find lots of types of bitters these days, and like liqueurs, they offer unique and different ways to add aligned magic to your lunar drinks. If using single-ingredient bitters, such as cherry or rhubarb bitters, you can look up the magical associations of that ingredient to understand what its aligned moon magic may be. However, if it is a proprietary blend, such as Angostura or Peychaud's bitters, it often includes a number of different ingredients that could be used for countless purposes.

Angostura

An old-fashioned and Manhattan would not be what they are without Angostura bitters. Contrary to what you might believe, these bitters do not contain the bark of the Angostura tree. Rather, this recipe was developed by the surgeon general of Simón Bolívar's army in Venezuela in 1824. Using over forty different ingredients, these aromatic bitters were designed to help with various maladies, particularly stomach ones, and took years to craft. The full recipe for these bitters is a highly guarded secret: Only a few people in the world know it.

Peychaud's

Anise-centric Peychaud's bitters were originally crafted by Haitian immigrant Antoine Amédée Peychaud in his New Orleans French Quarter apothecary in the 1830s. This Louisiana-brand recipe is what gave way to the Sazerac cocktail.

ALCOHOL, WATER, AND THE MOON

From the creation of Bach Flower Remedies to holy water, water has been used throughout the ages for healing, blessings, and magical enchantments. Beyond just being life giving, water has been shown by metaphysical researchers like Masaru Emoto to be able to hold on to an energetic vibration, an idea that both cultural and magical practices have utilized for years. People will often charge jars of water under the full moon to capture its energy—and you can actually do the same with your alcohol! In fact, most legally sold alcohols have water added to them. You can also use moon water in your concoctions through moon-charged ice cubes.

MIXOLOGY TOOLS

When it comes to mixing with the moon, having the right equipment makes the difference in crafting a powerful lunar elixir. The following are bartending tools you'll want to have on hand when mixing the recipes in Part 2.

- **Cocktail shaker:** A stainless steel cocktail shaker is a crucial element of any bartending kit. Professional bartenders generally prefer a stainless steel top with a matching stainless steel bottom, but there are kits available with glass bottoms. Ingredients are added with or without ice to the smaller half of the shaker, then covered with the top half before shaking. Shaking aerates a cocktail, adding volume and fizz, and shaking with ice waters down the beverage.
- **Jigger:** A jigger is important for measuring alcohol increments of 1 and $1^1/_2$ ounces. A jigger will often be double-sided for quick and efficient measuring.
- **Peeler:** A peeler is used to make garnishes from fruits.
- **Knife:** When flaming a peel as an exciting garnish, a knife is crucial as it allows for access to the white pith of the fruit, producing more essential oils to create a little flame.
- **Muddler:** A muddler squishes and mixes herbs and fresh ingredients in a concoction, allowing oils and juices to disperse into the beverage. A proper muddler is nice, but the back of a spoon can be used in a pinch.

- **Barspoon:** This is a long, usually stainless steel spoon that you will use to stir drinks and sometimes layer them. Its lengthy neck allows for a lot of easy, quick maneuvering in making cocktails. Sometimes a long spoon can be just as handy.
- **Strainers:** There are various strainers used in bartending to help remove solids from a finished beverage. For the recipes in this book, you can use Hawthorne and fine-mesh strainers. A Hawthorne strainer is a disc with two or more stabilizing prongs. A metal spring on the disc fits in the glass. The drink is then strained. A fine-mesh strainer has a mesh net to collect solids as a drink is poured over it.
- **Mixing glass:** This tool is truly optional. If you see yourself becoming a moon mixologist as a side hustle, it can be a worthwhile investment, but one-half of your cocktail shaker works just as well. You will use a mixing glass to easily stir drinks that contain ice, instead of shaking them, so that the resulting cocktails are still cold but not as aerated or frothy.

While there are many kinds of fancy equipment out there, you really only need a few tools to whip up deliciously enchanting drinks. Look into whatever options fit your budget.

GLASSWARE

When crafting your lunar libations, the glassware you choose can be just as important as the drink! A representation of life, and both a metaphorical and literal vessel for spirit, glassware can add aesthetics, aroma, and temperature to your drink. Just think of the mythical Holy Grail! The following list outlines the glassware used in Part 2.

- **Old-fashioned/rocks/bucket glass:** Holds 6–8 ounces; designed for building drinks directly in the glass.
- **Cocktail/martini glass:** Holds 3–5 ounces; designed for drinks mixed in a shaker and then strained into a glass without ice.
- **Highball/collins glass:** Holds 8–16 ounces; designed for tall drinks that often contain a larger amount of nonalcoholic mixers and are poured over ice.
- **Copper mug:** Holds 14–20 ounces; usually used for drinks like the Moscow Mule and mint julep.
- **Hurricane glass:** Holds 15–20 ounces; designed for tropical drinks like the piña colada.

- **Irish coffee glass:** Holds 6–12 ounces; designed of tempered glass for hot beverages.
- **Champagne flute:** Holds 6 ounces; designed for carbonated beverages.
- **Coupe glass:** Holds 4–6 ounces; designed for cocktails served "up" (shaken and strained without ice).
- **Red wine glass:** Holds 16–20 ounces; designed with a balloon-shaped bowl to release the aromas of the wine.
- **White wine glass:** Holds 8–12 ounces; designed with a slim bowl to preserve the temperature of chilled white wine.
- **Pint glass:** Holds 16 ounces; designed for beer but also often used for Blood Marys.

As with bartending tools, the glass options you select are up to you. Work with what is most accessible to you—and what calls out to you as you stir up your own delicious potions!

ELEMENTS OF MAGICAL BARTENDING

When it comes to mixing up moon-aligned cocktails, there are modern approaches that change the flavor and expression of your drink, and even add a bit of flair! The following are some terms and techniques used in bartending that can help you craft the most magical of moon mixes.

- **Shaking:** Shaking a cocktail (often with ice) in a cocktail shaker chills the drink, aerates it (giving it texture), and also dilutes it. Overall, shaking lends a more balanced and smoother finish to a cocktail.
- **Stirring:** An alternative to shaking, usually used with ingredients that are mostly made up of alcohol, stirring involves mixing your drink in a glass using a barspoon. Stirring dilutes and chills the drink, but less so than shaking, and does not aerate the drink. It allows for more of the alcohol element to shine through.
- **Pouring beer or sparkling wine:** When pouring beer or sparkling wine, it is best to tilt the glass at an angle, thereby allowing for only a modest amount of foam to appear on top. Magically, you can use this opportunity to visualize your life's cup filling up with blessings as the physical cup fills with liquid. Think of how the brewing goddess Ninkasi was believed to be contained in essence in every drop of beer.

- **Rimming**: Rimming a drink is the practice of adding a salt or sugar rim along the outside lip of a glass, typically for drinks like margaritas or lemon drop martinis. Magically, this is an opportunity to add extra alignments to your moon mixology, considering the protective qualities of salt and sweetening aspect of sugar. You can also mix a rim with other herbal ingredients. To rim a drink, cover the outside lip of the glass in citrus juice, either with a wedge or by dipping the lip into the juice. Then dip the lip in the desired ingredient until it sticks to the rim.
- **Straining and double straining**: Straining a drink occurs when a drink is not built in the drinking glass. It keeps out thick particles, unwanted ice shards, or partially melted ice from the finished drink. Oftentimes when a drink is shaken, it will be double strained using both the Hawthorne and mesh strainers to catch tiny spices, herbs, or ice shards.
- **Expressing**: Expressing a peel occurs when a citrus peel is squeezed over a drink to express its oils into the beverage. Sometimes the peel is then also rubbed around the rim of the glass to promote a citrus odor and taste when sipping.
- **Flaming**: To flame a peel, you simply express it over a lit match, thereby causing the oils of the citrus to briefly catch fire and add a smoky aroma to the peel, which is then added to the glass. This adds a bit of fire magic (associated with power and transformation) to your lunar libation.
- **Rinsing**: Rinsing a drink is done to line the inside of the glass with a particular alcohol, to lend it flavor but not overwhelm the beverage. To rinse a drink, place an ice cube or two in the glass, pour the smaller amount of alcohol over the cube, and let it sit. When you are ready to pour your drink in, rinse the glass by swirling it so the ice cubes move around the glass in a perfect circle with the alcohol, then shake it into the drain.
- **Dash**: A dash refers to an amount of bitters, specifically one drop. Bitters often have a spout that allows only one drop to leave the bottle at a time. Some lesser-known bitters will instead have a separate dropper you can use.
- **Chilling**: Chilling a glass helps keep your drink colder longer, rather than warming it up when you pour the drink in. You can chill a glass by keeping it in the freezer or filling it with ice cubes while you make the drink. Magically, you can use ice cubes made with moon water and add an enchanted rinse to your glass.

- **Building:** Building a drink means making a drink in the glass it will be sipped in. It requires no shaking: Simply add the ingredients to the final glass, add ice if indicated, then stir.
- **Garnishing:** Garnishes, while often underconsidered, are an important part of magical bartending. A well-thought-out garnish crafts an aroma that greets the nose as you sip, setting the tone of the drink. Magically, it's an opportunity to use organic aromatherapy. For example, for a drink that is meant to be calming, the fragrances of mint and lavender sprigs while you sip can completely transform the experience.

MOON MAGIC ON A BUDGET

The quality of the alcohol you use can make a big difference in both the taste of your drink and the aftereffects (the hangover—or absence of one!). The same goes for using fresh ingredients. However, it can be daunting to jump in and buy a big bottle of alcohol for a considerable price. The best thing is to find a sample-sized bottle to try first. Use this smaller size to taste a bit of the alcohol and experience its magical and mixology potential before committing to the cost of a larger bottle. You can also find many alternative mixology tools in your kitchen—such as the back of a wooden spoon for muddling or an ordinary glass for stirring—to use until you are ready to make an investment in specific equipment.

MIXING WITH THE MOON

Now that you know about the magical potential of each type of alcohol and the various tools, techniques, and mixology ingredient options out there, you are ready to start mixing...*almost*. First, you'll want to read the next chapter on moon basics, so you can make the most of each recipe in Part 2. In it, you'll uncover everything you need to know about the moon in order to create potent lunar cocktails on your own. You are one step closer to becoming a pro lunar mixologist!

CHAPTER 3

LUNAR BASICS

Ceaselessly changing form, the moon embodies mystery and transformation. Yes, the phases of the moon have been explained by science, but that doesn't lessen its mystical and enigmatic properties. In fact, there is a whole face of the moon you don't get to see from earth! Influencing the tides and perhaps even animal behavior and plant life, the various phases of the moon and occasional moons have many magical associations.

In this chapter, you will learn more about the potential of each moon for healing, magic, and transformation, from the luxuriant moon in Taurus to the fresh beginnings held by the new moon. This knowledge will provide the foundation for the lunar potions you mix up in Part 2. The enchanting world of the cosmos awaits!

PHASES OF THE MOON

There are four main phases of the moon: new, waxing, full, and waning. While this categorization can be broken down further, many astrologers believe that the new and full moons are the most important energetic markers of the lunar cycle and can still be energetically utilized one day before and after they occur. In the following sections, you'll explore each phase in more depth, uncovering the rituals, celebrations, and spells each phase is best suited for. Keep in mind that what you do—or don't do—with the potential of a phase is entirely up to you and what feels right in a given moment.

New Moon

A period when the moon does not reflect sunlight in the sky and thus isn't visible for up to three days, this phase marks the beginning of the lunar cycle. In some astrological practices, the moon is considered to be "new" right when it is aligned at 0 degrees with the sun. For this reason, on the day of the new moon, the moon will rise and set with the sun. However, to the human eye, the moon may appear new a day or so before this alignment, resulting in varying practices at this time. Some moon magicians use any of the three days for new moon magic, while others may use astrological calendars or online sources to practice on the exact day of the new moon. This book uses the 0-degree alignment for the new moon.

Since the new moon is in alignment with the sun, it will always be in the same sign that the sun is in. This alignment, also called a conjunction, makes the new moon a powerful time to focus on the energies highlighted by that sign. (You will learn more about the signs later in this chapter.) And considering that the moon will grow from this time forward, also known as waxing, this is a favorable time for new beginnings. This alignment is also the reason why a solar eclipse will only ever occur during a new moon.

With the moon unable to reflect the light of the sun, the world is left without the guidance of lunar light during the new moon. For some, this can symbolize a time to explore their shadow selves. To others, this time may feel more like a blank slate. Regardless, the new moon is undoubtedly a powerful occasion to work on setting intentions for things that you may want to increase in the future, whether it be money, confidence, or success. It presents an opportunity to realign yourself with, and also redefine, your goals.

As it is the start of a cycle, others view the new moon as an opportunity for rest and relaxation, or as a chance to prepare for manifesting and craft the proper foundation for new things to grow and prosper. So which route should you take in using the new moon's magic? Just like the moon changes from day to day, sometimes it is best to allow your own practices to change depending on how you are feeling. On some occasions, you may decide to use the alignment of the new moon for manifestation, while on other days, you may use it for shadow work.

Dark Moon

Some people recognize something called the "dark moon," the period right before the new moon. At this time, you cannot see any of the moon in the sky, but the moon has still not reached its 0-degree alignment with the sun. This is the liminal space—the space before life and death, where the rebirth of the new moon can be felt but not yet utilized or experienced. It is a space of limbo, and therefore it is a powerful energy of mystery and the cosmos. Many powerful moon deities rule this time. Some use the dark moon for deeply transformative inner work before rebirthing intentions with the new moon. For others, it is a key period of rest. Either way, this phase of the moon is a powerful time.

Note that some practitioners use the term *dark moon* to refer to the true new moon and the term *new moon* to refer to when you can see a sliver of the moon in the sky. If you use this definition, refer to the energy you desire or are seeking to guide your lunar libations in Part 2.

Waxing Moon

The waxing moon occurs when the moon begins to ascend from the shadows. This period represents a time of growth, abundance, and action. Each day, the moon will rise later and later in the day, until it finally rises at sundown on the night of the full moon. This is a time to reflect on following through with your intentions, as the pull of the moon can inspire and lend more energy to any endeavor. The waxing moon can be further separated into three subphases, each with a specific intention as well as different themes and challenges.

Waxing Crescent

The waxing crescent occurs when a sliver of the moon is visible, appearing as a backward C. This sliver of light can represent hope and faith and highlight themes of venturing into an unknown future. This is the first step of the moon on its path of growth, and it represents pursuing or following a dream. A time of newborn wonder and energy, it can also signify limitless possibilities, unknown potential, and personal drive.

First Quarter Moon

When the moon has waxed to form a half circle, it is known as the first quarter moon. On one hand, this can signify a time of balance. More has come to light with the first quarter moon, and now goals or ideas may face a stronger sense of realism. The first quarter moon can also be a time of crossroads and decision-making. As it moves from this halfway point, it can reflect a sense of tension or challenge. It is a time to push forward with your new moon intentions.

Waxing Gibbous

During the waxing gibbous phase, only a fragment of shadow remains. There may now be more confirmation of efforts made earlier in the lunation cycle. Results from intentions set during the new moon may begin to appear, and with them a sense of affirmation and optimism. With more of the moon illuminated, our own reality becomes illuminated as well. This could indicate an opportunity to further refine goals and intentions and narrow your focus. As any final hurdles are uncovered, the success of teamwork and cooperation may especially be highlighted during this time.

Full Moon

The full moon phase occurs when the moon is directly opposite (or in opposition to) the sun and fully reflects the sun's light. Queen of the night, the full moon will rise in the east as the sun sets and roam its domain until it sets in the west at sunrise. The full moon will always occur in the opposite zodiac sign from what the sun is in, an opposition that can spark tension or be used for balance and reflection.

The full moon's light, like a lighthouse in the dark sky, can be a source of energetic illumination and awakening, leading you to the shores of your emotions. Many moon worshippers see this as a time of extreme potency and power—a climax of energies. The full moon can thus be a powerful time for manifestation, amplifying intentions, and sending energy out into the world. On the other hand, some feel the full moon may be too energetically wild, or better utilized for release and forgiveness in conjunction with the waning moon. The full moon is also a celebration of harvest and culmination. For some in the astrological community, it is a reminder of endings, for from the full moon onward, the moon will wane in strength until the cycle begins anew. This gives an opportunity for release and realization.

Waning Moon

The waning moon period occurs when the light reflected by the moon slowly decreases, until the moon is no longer visible in the sky. As the image of the waning light might insinuate, this is a time of decrease and is potent for gratitude, sharing, forgiveness, banishment, and endings. This is the time to focus on anything you wish to lessen in your life, such as bad habits, or whatever issues the full moon may have highlighted.

While the full moon represents a climax, the period that follows is a reflection on endings. It brings wisdom and humility. The waning moon period can further be divided into three subphases: the waning gibbous; the third, or last quarter moon; and the waning crescent.

Waning Gibbous

During the waning gibbous phase, a slow and soft shadow grows on the moon. This is a time when you may still reap the benefits of any moon manifestation work or intentions you set. To some, this moon is a moon of gratitude and sharing. It may be a time to share knowledge with others as you enter into a more reflective phase, and to show appreciation for the work that has been done.

Third/Last Quarter Moon

The third quarter moon occurs when the moon is once again at 50 percent illumination. This is a return to the darker part of the moon's cycle and is a time of graceful endings. As an energetic pivot point, it may cultivate a calm release of energy or, through tension, show where energy still needs to be released. This is an especially powerful occasion for fully letting go and forgiving, for cutting ties. Similarly, it can be a time of creative expression.

Waning Crescent

The waning crescent occurs when the moon passes its third quarter phase and is now darker than it is bright. The end of the lunar cycle looms. This is truly a time of surrender and release, as the ending is now undeniable. During the waning crescent, wrap things up and put to rest any lingering concerns in order to prepare for rebirth with the new moon.

MOON PHASES

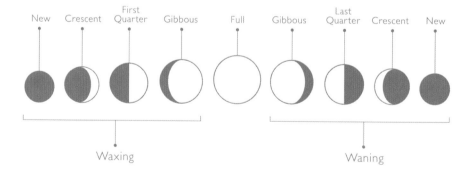

OCCASIONAL MOONS

Beyond the moon phases, there are occasional lunar events that are particularly powerful. The various eclipses and blue and black moons can help craft extraordinary moon magic.

Eclipses

Eclipses typically occur multiple times each year. They are the culmination of particular placements of the moon, sun, and earth that obstruct either the moon or sun from our view. These events, known as solar or lunar eclipses, craft an intense coupling of transformative energy. They can allow for deep and profound healing. Additionally, these eclipses often mark an energetic pattern or cycle that can last six months or more.

Solar Eclipse

Solar eclipses occur when the moon aligns between the earth and sun, blocking the sun from view on earth. Hence, a solar eclipse can only occur during a new moon, with the sun and moon in the same sign. Due to the moon's (and thus its shadow's) relatively small size compared to the earth, a solar eclipse at its max will only last a few minutes or even seconds. There are three types of solar eclipses: partial, in which the moon does not pass completely in front of the sun, leaving a crescent of the sun still visible; annular, in which the moon is farthest in its elliptical orbit around the earth, and thus leaves a halo of light around the sun; and total, in which the moon completely covers the sun.

Solar eclipses are a meeting of the two most dynamic and powerful celestial bodies relative to earth. On a magical level, this opportunity can be used to reflect on matters of balance, of the sun and moon meeting in a perfect instance. While some practitioners feel that eclipses are energetically chaotic, unpredictable, and best left magically untapped, others say they are powerful times for manifestation.

As a new moon, it is a time of new beginnings and can initiate new life paths. Use the time to move through obstacles and tap into a new perspective to help you do so. Look into what sign the moon will be in for the eclipse, to better understand its particular energy. When choosing a concoction from Part 2 for this endeavor, you can select a new moon cocktail related to that moon, or one connected to the solar eclipse. Also look at what sign the accompanying lunar eclipse(s) may be in, to help provide greater context for the energetic themes that the eclipse season is tied to.

Lunar Eclipse

A lunar eclipse occurs during a full moon, when the earth is placed directly between the moon and sun. The earth's shadow casts darkness or discoloration and blocks out the rays of sun from the moon.

There are three types of lunar eclipses: penumbral, partial, and total. A penumbral eclipse is a partial and very subtle eclipse that occurs when the moon is in the secondary shadow of the earth, called the penumbra. At times, such an eclipse may not even be visible. A partial lunar eclipse occurs when the moon is in the main part of the earth's shadow, known as the umbra, and the color of a portion of the moon changes. A total lunar eclipse occurs when the moon is completely inside the earth's umbra. The moon does not completely black out or disappear, but it does have strong and striking coloration. The total lunar eclipse is the longest eclipse, lasting for more than an hour and a half.

Given that lunar eclipses occur during a full moon in the opposite sign of the sun, they are essentially a supercharged full moon. They can add an extra element of wildness and emotionality and can therefore be powerful vehicles for healing and change. By bringing to the surface hidden emotions, lunar eclipses can shed a light on old wounds or shadows. They can mark big changes in relationships and the external world. The energy of a lunar eclipse can inspire change that can affect us for the following six months or longer. Pay attention to your emotions around this time, as well as what sign the moon is in during the eclipse, to help further reveal what energy may be at play for you.

As with solar eclipses, some believe lunar eclipses to be times of erratic, unpredictable energy and thus not times to do manifestation work. Some disagree, however, and use the rarity and immense power of the eclipse for miracle-like magic. Again, this can depend entirely on you and what's happening in your life. If you feel particularly emotionally activated, then use the time for deep healing, illumination, reflection, and change. If the lunar eclipse has energized you mentally or physically, perhaps focus more on things you wish to bring into your life, then do some lunar manifestation magic.

Blue Moon

Because the moon's cycle is 29.5 days, and most months are thirty or thirty-one days long, every three years or so there are two full moons in one month. The second of these full moons within a calendar month is referred to as a blue moon. This type of blue moon is the result of merging a lunar cycle with a mostly solar-oriented calendar and differs from an astrological blue moon, which is mentioned later in this section. The blue moon can be a powerful time for manifestation and can certainly induce a sense of wonder, magic, and chance. As the result of combining the natural moon with the human-made calendar, a blue moon can also be used as a time of alchemy and self-made success. A blue moon's energies will largely depend on the sign that it is in, but it can also be used as a time to put extra focus in a particular area and for do-overs.

Astrologically, a blue moon is a moon that occurs for the second time within one zodiacal sign, such as if two full moons occur in Gemini, rather than one. In such a circumstance, reflect on what is happening in the skies in that moment. For example, those two Gemini full moons in one period can be an important pattern of healing and repetition.

Black Moon

The term *black moon* is used to refer to the second new moon within a month. Such a moon may occur every twenty-nine months or so, and then only during a thirty-one-day month. However, an alternative or other definition is the third new moon in an astronomical season, and this can occur every thirty-three months or so. Like the blue moon, black moons can provide emphasis in a certain area of your life, and given the power of new moons for new beginnings, this is a powerful time to use energy for a fresh start.

Supermoon

Although the term *supermoon* certainly connotes a sense of powerfulness, supermoons are a more regular occurrence than blue and black moons. Supermoons occur when a full moon is closest to the earth in its elliptical orbit. That means the moon appears significantly larger. Due to this increased closeness and luminescence, some people may feel an increased connection to and stronger energetic pull from the supermoon. Thus, it may make doing lunar magic easier, or inspire enhanced emotions and power.

MONTHLY MOONS

Beyond its consistent cycle of 29.5 days, the moon has served as a marker of the passage of time in additional ways throughout history. As a way to describe seasonal changes and a moon's particular magic or ethereal glow, many cultures designated the full moons of each month with specific names and connotations. It is important to recognize and acknowledge that some of the names we commonly use today to describe different moons come from Indigenous tribes in North America. Names like *harvest* or *seed moon* reflected certain themes and areas of wisdom and focus. To this day, farmers and gardeners alike heed the various monthly full moons in their cultivation practices, and many nature-oriented spiritualists use these moons as a way to guide their healing, manifestation, and other magical practices.

However, since the moon's cycle does not perfectly line up with our modern solar-based calendar, this has resulted in varying names for the monthly moons. In the following sections, you will learn about the various monthly full moons that many use to guide their lunar practices. Combining the lunar associations of these moons with themes you witness around you and the astrological sign the moon is in can help you cultivate an utterly magical and transformative experience. Do note that in the Southern Hemisphere, the seasonal associations of a particular moon are for the month opposite the one indicated in this section. For example, April is a marker of fall in the Southern Hemisphere, and its moon's names and meanings in this hemisphere are more aligned with the Northern Hemisphere's September or October moon.

January Full Moon

The first moon of the new year, the January full moon is also called the cold, ice, winter, and wolf moon and represents beginnings, strength, courage, and healing. In snowy climates and also during the winter holidays, people are locked inside with their families, and survival can rely upon these bonds. That makes this moon a good time for relationship-bonding work and also for ancestral healing and reflection. The January full moon also follows the winter solstice and thus is a good time for new ventures and projects.

February Full Moon

The February full moon, otherwise known as the chaste, quickening, storm, wild, and wolf moon, is a time of cleansing, new beginnings, and fertility. With the combination of Pisces and Aquarius sun energies that cushion this moon, it is a period of connecting to one's inner child and the simplicity within that space. And after the introspective winter, it is a good time to shed any revealed thoughts and ideas that may be limiting to your life's journey. It is a moon of innovation, imagination, empowerment, astral work, and boundless ideas.

March Full Moon

Also known as the chaste, raven, seed, storm, and windy moon, the March full moon ushers in prosperity, fertility, and success. All life is buzzing with energy as nature begins to not just grow, but flourish. It is a moon of action, harmony, and movement. With boundless energy and ideas, it is also a great moon for creativity and inspiration. This is a good time to bless and plant seeds for future growth, whether personal, financial, or business related.

April Full Moon

Also known as the hare, seed, flower, planter's, meadow, and windy moon, the April full moon heralds a time of beginnings, fertility, and growth. All of nature is in full movement at this time, and there is a very nurturing energy in the air. And now that nature is in reproductive mode, it is also a good time for lust and romance.

May Full Moon

Nature is in full swing at the time of the May full moon. Also known as the fairy, flower, goddess, hare, milk, and dyad moon, this moon welcomes or follows the sabbat Beltane, also known as May Day. The May full moon is a time of more fertility and also well-being and love.

June Full Moon

The June full moon greets the coming summer season. Also called the dyad, green, corn, mead, partner, rose, strawberry, and honey moon, the June full moon is a time to celebrate and invoke abundance, prosperity, love, and marriage. Occurring in the sweet spot between spring and summer, there is a particular heat to this moon that invokes a sense of hard work, manifestation, and romance.

July Full Moon

In the middle of summer, along with Cancer and Leo season, the July full moon is a time of completion. As its alternative names like blessing, herb, mead, and summer moon might suggest, many herbs are ready to be cut during this moon. But this harvest season is both external and internal: The July moon is a key time to work on karmic ties and past lives as well as spiritual endeavors. This is an opportunity to connect the dots in your internal patterns and nurture your spiritual self to continue to evolve and transcend.

August Full Moon

By the August full moon, harvest season is approaching. Also known as the barley, corn, fruit, herb, and wort moon, this is a moon where the coming harvest is celebrated. Therefore, this is a great moon for abundance and prosperity workings. Additionally, there is something to be said for the fact that every grain harvested offers a seed that can be resown to sprout in the spring. It is a symbolic time to contemplate rebirth and continue working on energetic ties, particularly those related to familial matters and patterns.

September Full Moon

Known as the barley, harvest, nut, and wine moon, the September full moon coincides with the grape harvest season. For this reason, this moon is associated with the higher self, internal wisdom, and psychic development, which were associated with wine's effects in some ancient cultures. It is also a time to turn one's eye to protection magic, preparing the home for winter and doing any last manifestation spells before harvest season ends.

October Full Moon

Known as the blood, harvest, and hunter's moon, the October full moon comes toward the end of the hunting and harvest season and is a time to reflect on the repeating cycle of life, death, and rebirth. Soon all life on earth will begin to recede into the cocoon of winter. This is a good moon for giving thanks, giving "death" or release to bad habits and thoughts, separation, and any efforts that involve opening the doorway to allow for a new beginning. It is also an opportunity for physical healing efforts, honoring memories, and stability.

November Full Moon

The November full moon, also known as the beaver, larder, mourning, snow, and white moon, ushers in the hibernation season of winter. All life is taking a metaphorical nap, and energy becomes dormant and internalized. The November full moon is a good time for efforts that involve tying up loose ends, completing old projects, and practicing cooperation—all to allow for a comfortable winter. It is also a good time to create space for the reinvention of yourself and your life.

December Full Moon

The December full moon, also known as the long night, oak, and snow moon, is a moon of balance, confidence, and new beginnings. With its proximity to the winter solstice, the longest night of the year, it symbolizes the restoration of balance in the universe, and the growing energy of the sun from this time forward can be utilized for aspirations, strength, self-confidence, prosperity, and new beginnings. It is also a good moon to release any remaining obstacles and stagnancy.

SEASONAL TRANSITIONS

Throughout the year, there are various astronomical events, as well as some pagan-based holidays, that have turned into what is called the Wheel of the Year. The Wheel of the Year reflects seasonal changes and themes in tune with nature and our experiences with life on earth. These events correspond to different moon phases and can be utilized for powerful magic.

Spring Equinox

Sometimes referred to as Ostara, the spring equinox is the day when the hours of light and darkness are held in equal balance for a brief moment of time. It also marks the start of spring. Coming out of winter, it represents a reemergence and the beginning of the astrological year. Life is abuzz, and all is growing in abundance. From this day forth, the hours of daylight will surpass the hours of darkness, and so many efforts will increase. The spring equinox correlates with the first quarter moon, since both connect to this moment of balance followed by a theme of increase.

Beltane

Beltane, also known as May Day, is the cross-quarter day between the spring equinox and the summer solstice. In the middle of spring, it celebrates growth as well as a zest for life. It is a time of excitement, increase, and sensuality. This day corresponds to the waxing gibbous moon, which is also a time of growth and excitement.

Summer Solstice

The summer solstice, sometimes called Litha in pagan and witchcraft practices, is a time when daylight is at its longest. From this day forth, the daylight will slowly wane. With the sun at its maximum power, the summer solstice correlates to the full moon. It is a time of culmination, power, and manifestation.

Lammas/Lughnasadh

Lammas is the first of the three harvests and is a cross-quarter day marking the halfway point between the summer solstice and fall equinox. It correlates to the waning gibbous moon, with themes of gratitude, sharing, celebration of bounty, and blessings still to come. It also marks the start of endings and of sacrifice.

Fall Equinox

The fall equinox, sometimes referred to as Mabon by the pagan community, is a time of equal daylight and dark hours, like the spring equinox. However, from this day forward, the darker hours will exceed the hours of light. This day also accompanies the transition of seasons from summer to fall, acting as a gateway to themes of loss, letting go, death, and transformation. This day corresponds to the third quarter moon, which also holds a momentary balance of equal light and dark.

Samhain

Traditionally the cross-quarter day between the fall equinox and winter solstice, Samhain marks the third harvest and final transition from light to dark. The hours of darkness are now longer than the hours of light. As the final harvest of the season, it is a time of bounty but also of loss and letting go. Many cultures across the world worship the dead at this time. This day corresponds to the waning crescent moon, during which the moon's light is barely a sliver in the sky.

Winter Solstice

Also known as Yule, the winter solstice is the longest night of the year. Since from this day forward, the light will slowly grow again, this is often viewed as a day of rebirth and hope. Similarly, it corresponds to the meaning of the new moon; although you may not see the moon in the sky, from that day forward, the light will grow.

Imbolc

Imbolc celebrates the middle of winter, and forthcoming return of spring. Traditionally, it may have been treated as a cross-quarter day, but today many in the Northern Hemisphere celebrate it around February 2, a date soon after the lunar new year, which is also a time of resetting. It is a day that celebrates the inevitable change ahead from winter to spring, eagerly beckoning the daylight to return. This day corresponds to the waxing crescent and similarly represents themes of hope and pursuit.

ASTROLOGICAL SIGNS AND THE MOON

Astrological signs are based on the general position of the sun and stars relative to the earth at the time of your birth. But while many people known their sun signs, very few know their moon signs. Yes, the moon (and every astrological body) was also in a given constellation during your birth.

Beyond the various phases, the astrological sign the moon is in at a given time plays a role in the powers and themes connected to that moon, and it can impact how you choose to utilize it. In particular, the sign of a new or full moon reflects strong energies that can become the focus of the entire month. In the following sections, you will explore the various astrological placements and their effects on the moon and your magic workings. These sections include date ranges for when the new and full moons will be in a given sign.

ARIES: March 21–April 19

Symbolized by the ram, Aries ushers in the astrological season with brute force and vigor. Ruled by the planet Mars of action and war, along with the passionate element of fire, Aries trailblazes with its impulsivity and ready-to-go attitude. While this can be great for initiating projects, breaking through obstacles, and passion, this energy can also be reckless and devolve into tunnel vision. This ambitious sign can lead to becoming a little overly focused on reaching a goal, no matter the cost. Aries also offers energy great for physicality, such as exercise, handwork, and athletic competitions.

Moon in Aries

Following its nature as the first sign of the zodiac, Aries takes charge like a ram and brings about change and a willingness to spring into action. The moon in Aries is an opportunity to reflect on themes of courage, leadership, and victory. Its motivational energy can give you the push needed to get things done and tie up loose ends. The Aries moon can also be a good time to face the things you may otherwise avoid, and inspires impulsiveness. It is great for magical efforts and intentions around competition, physicality, and one's personal needs.

- **New Moon in Aries (March 21–April 19):** This new moon is the first of the zodiac and welcomes spring, making it an ultrapowerful moon for new beginnings and starting the season off with invigoration and passion. Use this new moon to emphasize the initiatory aspect of Aries.
- **Full Moon in Aries (September 23–October 22):** This moon marks the end of a six-month cycle set forth by the Aries new moon, so if you have a lunar journal, you may want to reflect back and see how themes have changed or been amplified since the new moon. While the full moon does signify a time of completion, the full moon in Aries can really spark a strong sense of courage and leadership to pursue one's goals—or perhaps warrant a lot of short-tempered, outlandish, and fiery emotions if not intentionally directed and utilized.

TAURUS: April 20–May 20

Following Aries is steadfast Taurus. This grounded earth sign brings an energy of stability and comfort; it's a hardworking, reliable, and practical energy great for laying lasting foundations. The symbol of the bull has been worshipped in various cultures as a sign of wealth, potency, and security, all themes Taurus can relate to. However, this sign is also ruled by Venus (the embodiment of beauty, pleasure, and love), leading it to be a sensual, luxury-loving sign. At times, this can mean leaning into health and practicing self-care. However, at other times, this can mean turning an occasional comfort into a daily indulgence or laziness.

Moon in Taurus

The Taurus moon brings a focus to wealth, stability, and overall enjoyment of earthly pleasures. Attentions are called to the home environment and to establishing a sense of security and a safe foundation. This theme of security extends to finances and long-term planning as well. This is also a time to enjoy physical pleasures and embrace sensuality as well as lasting connections and intimacy in relationships.

- **New Moon in Taurus (April 20–May 20):** The new moon in earth-oriented Taurus presents the perfect opportunity to plant seeds for wealth and long-term relationships and to establish a balance of healthy habits and indulgence. The Taurus moon can be a time to turn attention to the home as a place of enjoyment and a foundation upon which success can grow.
- **Full Moon in Taurus (October 23–November 21):** The steadfast Taurus full moon amid ever-changing Scorpio season brings a focus to the balance between security and transformation. It is a good time to reflect on your habits and make sure you are in balance with your productivity and relaxation, and also with money and romance. Taurus is a long-term relationship sign, so the full moon in Taurus can be a particularly romantic one for these relationships, or for sensuality and physical pleasures. It is also great for manifesting wealth and encouraging physical health through eating and exercise.

GEMINI: May 21–June 20

Symbolized by the twins, Gemini can embody complexity and fickleness. This constant duality allows for entertainment, versatility, curiosity, and gathering information. Ruled by Mercury (the planet of communication, travel, and technology), and an intelligent air sign, Gemini represents all things expression, whether through conversation, via writing, or even electronically in the workplace. The association with Mercury compounded by Gemini's excited, moving energy means this is also a great sign for travel.

Moon in Gemini

The moon in Gemini, with its symbolism of the twins, offers the perfect time to reflect on communication, especially within relationships, and the push and pull between how one feels and how one is perceived. This time is also potent for communicating oneself to others, especially in matters of business and receiving recognition. The airiness of Gemini combined with the luminous and transformative powers of the moon offers a key time to invoke inspiration for solving problems, coming up with new and unique ideas, or making powerful and exciting connections.

- **New Moon in Gemini (May 21–June 20):** Since Gemini is a sign that loves communication and all that comes with it, this can a powerful time to start a new way of connecting. Think about how well you are communicating with people: Are you being honest? Expressing yourself the way you would like to? This moon can also be perfect for those seeking creative pursuits or hoping to gather information. Some may experience mental overload during this time, in which case working on your relationship with your own mind is key. Meditation can help soothe the mind and organize thoughts and ideas. Sibling relationships may be highlighted at this time, so reflect on your sibling(s) or sibling dynamics.
- **Full Moon in Gemini (November 22–December 21):** The full moon in Gemini could inspire a wealth and influx of ideas and urges. If the full moon inspires you to socialize in some way, know that information you receive at this time could be particularly energizing and motivating. At the same time, in opposition to higher-purpose-oriented Sagittarius, this moon could highlight issues of balance among personal values, truth, gossip, and communication. This full moon is also good for receiving recognition for ideas and personal genius. Use the waning period after the full moon to release issues around overthinking and communication.

CANCER: June 21–July 22

Symbolized by the crab, which values the hard shell that protects its soft inner world, Cancer brings a central focus to the home. It is an opportunity for vulnerability and comfort. This sign can also be protective and nurturing toward others, which can develop into codependency if you are not careful. Ruled by the moon (the embodiment of emotions and the subconscious) and the emotional, perceptive water element, this sign is also intuitive, healing, and focused on spiritual development.

Moon in Cancer

The only sign directly ruled by the moon, Cancer inspires a focus on psychic development, emotions, and nurturance. As the firm shell of the soft crab may indicate, having a strong home or foundation is important for emotional safety and vulnerability and thus the healing the moon in Cancer often drives us to find. In its home sign of Cancer, this moon can also be a powerful opportunity for inner journeying, emotional power, and introspection. Compared to its opposite on the zodiac, Capricorn, Cancer is focused on goals arising from the self for personal development. Aspirations from the heart for inner fulfillment take center stage during the moon in Cancer.

- **New Moon in Cancer (June 21–July 22):** The Cancer new moon is a key time for new beginnings with emotions, spiritual development, personal goals, and give-and-take balances within relationships. Use this time to establish a new level of care and closeness with those you want to deepen your relationships with, or utilize this new moon to care more for yourself. Take the time to tend to your home environment to make it a safe and comfortable space for healing.
- **Full Moon in Cancer (December 22–January 19):** The full moon in Cancer greets the entry into the new year. Emotions tend to rise to the surface during full moons, and the Cancer moon amplifies this even more, offering an opportunity to set a new emotional balance. Being a sign that deals with the home environment and psychic abilities, Cancer under its ruling body (the moon) is a particularly powerful time to check in with these areas.

LEO: July 23–August 22

Following protective and nurturing Cancer comes flamboyant and enthusiastic Leo. Ruled by the sun—which represents the fullest expression of oneself as well as creativity and happiness—and the energetic, passionate fire element, this sign can highlight a time to be the center of one's own universe. Symbolized by the lion, it is a sign of pride and ego but also immense creativity and confidence. This is a great sign for performers and attracting attention. This is also a time for having fun and connecting with others in that generous and loyal Leo spirit.

Moon in Leo

When the moon travels through sun-ruled Leo, it is a time for self-expression and socialization/parties. The Leo moon offers an opportunity to reflect on and fine-tune how to express yourself in the world and how to shine as brightly as the full moon itself! At times, this can mean heart-centered leadership, while at others, it can mean embodying some glamour and self-devotion. Given that Leo is a creative, playful, and expressive sign, this is also an excellent time to connect to the moon for creativity and divine inspiration. Use this time to reinvent yourself, have fun with friends and explore new relationships, and imbue yourself with a bit more confidence.

- **New Moon in Leo (July 23–August 22):** Looking for a fresh start in self-expression, leadership, creativity, positivity, or fame? The new moon in Leo is the perfect time to achieve this! As Leo is a sign of ingenuity, guardianship, passion, recognition, and optimism, this new moon is a key time to work on manifesting a newfound sense of self—or just to pamper yourself in true Leo fashion!
- **Full Moon in Leo (January 20–February 18):** The full moon in Leo is a great time for gaining attention, channeling lunar creativity, and getting flirtatious. Use the time to brush up on your enchanting and romantic skills, to draw down the moon for recognition, and to embody more confidence and boldness. Occurring opposite the Aquarius sun, this moon will also highlight balances or conflicts between individuality and identity within group situations.

VIRGO: August 23–September 22

Infamous for a critical energy, Virgo season offers a key opportunity for discernment and details. Symbolized by the maiden and ruled by Mercury, the planet of communication, travel, and technology, Virgo is a service-oriented sign, so this is a great time to connect with community. Often depicted carrying grains, the maiden can represent the harvest as well as handwork and labor. A stable earth sign, it can be utilized for analyzing efficiency, keeping busy, and creating structure and organization.

Moon in Virgo

A sign of productivity, acuity, and function, Virgo invites you to analyze your life, and with the moon in this sign, this is a key opportunity to declutter—physically *and* emotionally—and to set in place better systems, whether in business, finances, daily habits, or health. Virgo is often perceived as nitpicky, but like all things under the sun (or moon), it has its space. The moon in Virgo illuminates things in your life that no longer serve you. You may also feel called to reflect on ways you are of service to others or your community.

- **New Moon in Virgo (August 23–September 22):** The Virgo new moon bodes the coming of fall in the Northern Hemisphere and spring in the Southern Hemisphere. On either side, the new moon in Virgo offers an opportunity for checks and balances—to discern what is and isn't efficient and helpful in your life—and to focus on details and organization. This could mean physical organization and cleaning, or analyzing your habits and even beliefs. And whether it be with your sense of greater purpose in life or through serving your community, contemplate new attempts you can make, no matter how small, to help others.
- **Full Moon in Virgo (February 19–March 20):** For the moon sensitive, the Virgo full moon can feel overwhelming and anxious, like there is too much to do or organize. If this applies to you, this moon can really be a good time to focus on resting and letting go. However, this energy can also be channeled efficiently into other areas. Being a full moon, a time of culmination and illumination, it can be powerful for intentions of health, habits, routines, and work, and for reflections on matters of community service. The Virgo moon amid watery Pisces season also highlights the need for balance between structure and flexibility.

LIBRA: September 23–October 22

Following critical Virgo comes harmony-oriented Libra season. Symbolized by the scales, this is a sign of balance and justice. A communicative air sign ruled by Venus (the planet of beauty, pleasure, and love), Libra has the ability to see all sides, making it a great sign for charming, socializing, and invoking harmony. It also lends itself to artistic endeavors and understanding complexity and truth in art.

Moon in Libra

The moon in Libra is a time to reflect and bring balance to all matters. Guiding you to view all perspectives, the Libra moon can invite deeper relationships with others, encouraging you to solve problems in favor of cooperation and mutual understanding. It is also a time to work on issues around justice and equality. With its influence from Venus coupled with the focus on exploring matters from all sides, this moon presents an opportunity for diving into the arts, spiritual and physical beauty, and empathic connections or romance.

- **New Moon in Libra (September 23–October 22):** The new moon in Libra offers a potent and magical opportunity to cultivate a new sense of equilibrium in your life. Whether it be in your relationships with yourself, others, or the world at large, now is the time to focus on where you need more balance and to set intentions on what that balance might look like. Additionally, Venus brings pleasure, so focus on how to indulge or start a new self-care regime.
- **Full Moon in Libra (March 21–April 19):** With the full moon in Libra and the sun in Aries, this can be an especially romantic and pleasure-filled time. Use the power of this full moon to deepen romantic connections, change up your look for a bit of glamour, or practice some self-care. At the same time, similar to the new moon, the Libra full moon will bring focus to balance within your life, especially between personal urges and consideration for others. It may also highlight areas of indecision.

SCORPIO: October 23–November 21

Symbolized by the scorpion with its sharp tail, Scorpio craves intensity, digging deep into all matters in search of intimacy and the heart of any issue, person, or situation. Being an intuitive and emotional water sign ruled by Pluto (the planet of death, destruction, and rebirth), this sign has a very healing and transformative energy and often inspires reflections on sensuality as well as life-and-death experiences. With its deep understanding and intensity, Scorpio is also great for money, strategizing, and understanding how a single word or action can curate a favorable outcome.

Moon in Scorpio

A powerful, raw energy that dives deep for personal growth and transformation, the Scorpio moon can initiate profound and immense change. Ultimately, this moon is about facing the ego in search of truth. This is a good time to explore sexuality, investigate the rawness of life and death though passion and intimacy, further your psychic development and divination regarding personal growth, and initiate reflection on the need for personal change.

- **New Moon in Scorpio (October 23–November 21):** Scorpio inspects deep-rooted insecurities, fears, and other shadow-related themes for healing and transformation. The new moon in Scorpio is a key time to investigate these issues for a fresh start, letting go of grudges and old wounds in pursuit of inner peace. It's no surprise that the Scorpio new moon is also a time to get a bit sexy and mysterious, and to deepen intimacy in relationships of all kinds—just be sure to respect boundaries! Finally, the Scorpio new moon presents an opportunity for improved finances, particularly within financial partnerships.
- **Full Moon in Scorpio (April 20–May 20):** Occurring during secure, comfort-seeking Taurus season, the Scorpio full moon can definitely poke and prod psyches out of their comfort zones and encourage exploration into the unknown. This full moon is also prone to illuminate more negative emotions such as jealousy, fear, and cruelness in order to facilitate deeper healing. Not to mention it can be a particularly erotic moon!

SAGITTARIUS: November 22–December 21

Ruled by Jupiter, which represents how one relates to the world at large and invokes abundance and good fortune, Sagittarius is an expansive sign, overseeing freedom and new opportunities. This energetic fire sign often invokes excitement and spontaneity. Represented by the archer with their arrow pointed in search of new horizons, Sagittarius always seeks the new, optimistic in search of expansion. It is also a sign focused on prophecy and meaning, reflecting on beliefs and ideas that affect the way we see the world and find meaning within it.

Moon in Sagittarius

The moon in Sagittarius leads to pursuits of a "higher nature"—philosophies, knowledge, belief systems, and a personal sense of purpose. At times, the questions this moon sets forth can inspire education that expands your horizons and sense of possibility. The moon in Sagittarius also prompts a sense of celebration, and its planetary rulership from Jupiter can promote luck, optimism, and expansion.

- **New Moon in Sagittarius (November 22–December 21):** The new moon in Sagittarius is a great time to adopt new life perspectives and optimism. Known for its scholarly side and spontaneity, the Sagittarius new moon is boundless, prompting free thought surrounding belief systems. Use the new moon in this sign to start a new dedication to studies or to being more inquisitive or positive. If there are big questions that have been looming in your life, let them lead you into a new perception of the world around you. But do not forget to have fun, take risks, and laugh!
- **Full Moon in Sagittarius (May 21–June 20):** The full moon in Sagittarius can certainly be an energizing one, inspiring a sense of impulsiveness, spiritual insights, and fiery fun. Use this time to explore what perspectives or old beliefs you may need to let go of, to ask big life questions, and to gain illumination. At the same time, this moon may prompt a desire for adventure: Be sure to follow that urge and enjoy the ride!

CAPRICORN: December 22–January 19

Ruled by Saturn, the planet of responsibility and restraint as well as opportunities and good fortune, and represented by the sturdy sea goat, Capricorn is a sign focused on structures—familial, institutional, physical, and otherwise. This season can bring success, helping you understand or create the structures needed to build a career or a family unit, or to succeed in a variety of situations. It symbolizes the wisdom that comes from these dynamics, but at the same time, it can reveal rigidity. A dependable, hardworking earth sign, Capricorn can build lasting structures.

Moon in Capricorn

The moon in headstrong Capricorn is a powerful time for reflection and evaluation of matters of efficiency, power, traditions and value systems, discipline, and focus. The Capricorn moon presents the opportunity to either seek the wisdom of traditional systems and family or to change these systems if they no longer serve you. This moon can also be used to establish or reflect on matters of self-control. Do you have the discipline, focus, and strategy with which to achieve your goals? Additionally, it is a good time to reorganize your finances and do some money manifesting.

- **New Moon in Capricorn (December 22–January 19):** Capricorn is notorious for having a plan, so it should be no surprise that the new moon in this sign invites the perfect opportunity for preparation. As an earth sign, Capricorn is all about planting seeds for long into the future. The new moon in Capricorn can also be the perfect opportunity to embrace a sense of ambition and renewed energy and add those qualities to your life. Additionally, it may be an ideal time to establish new goals and set forth new structures and systems within your life to achieve these goals.
- **Full Moon in Capricorn (June 21–July 22):** The full moon in Capricorn can be a powerful time for a burst of confidence and ambition to aid in achieving previously set goals and financial pursuits. Occurring opposite the sun in Cancer, this moon calls for a balance between ambitions and self-care, between being controlling and caring for others. Have your own goals, but do not be so blinded by them that you lose care and compassion for yourself or others.

AQUARIUS: January 20–February 18

Ruled by Uranus, the revolutionary, radical planet, Aquarius brings the unexpected. Seeing beyond the red tape and outside the box Capricorn works hard to craft, Aquarius is the rebel, helping to invite in new perspectives and innovation. Above all, this is a sign of personal freedom and liberation, inviting you to rip off old labels and ideas set forth by society in search of your own personal truth. Symbolized by the water bearer, Aquarius is actually an air sign, encouraging keen intelligence and communication skills.

Moon in Aquarius

Marked by innovation, the Aquarius moon offers an opportunity to reflect on how you label yourself individually and within your collective community. While labels can help you explore and understand yourself, they can also be confining, and the Aquarius moon is a time to reflect on ways you have outgrown such labels. Such questioning may lead you to reinvent yourself and reimagine the realm of what you see as possible.

- **New Moon in Aquarius (January 20–February 18):** The Aquarius new moon provides the perfect chance for a fresh start, detached from energy currents of the past. This moon invites you to examine your emotional ties and act freely of them, should you choose to. Use the Aquarius new moon to be true to yourself or to connect to your sense of individuality and quirkiness. This can also be a great time to inspire some innovation in your life or to think outside the box. Aquarius is also drawn to humanitarianism, so use the new moon to reflect on any activism, charity, or revolutionary work you feel called to.
- **Full Moon in Aquarius (July 23–August 22):** The Aquarius full moon, occurring in ebullient Leo season, can highlight issues of identity within social circles. The bright Aquarius full moon can certainly inspire innovation and a connection with your unique identity, but it can also simultaneously call attention to where you feel restricted in your outer world. There may be a need for more balance between detachment and relationships—between the head and the heart.

PISCES: February 19–March 20

Ruled by Neptune, the planet of dreams and illusions, Pisces swims deep in the water of human consciousness—and subconsciousness. As a water sign, this fish can struggle to separate from emotions. At times, this can bring deep healing, imagination, and compassion. However, it can also highlight a need for boundaries. Pisces can teach you to go with the flow, trust your inner guidance, and dream in a healthy way.

Moon in Pisces

The moon in Pisces provides a powerful opportunity to delve deep into the self, spirituality and the psychic realm, untapped dreams and aspirations, healing, and artistic inspiration. The Pisces moon is all about going with the flow, and its calming and cooling energy makes it favorable for peaceful resolutions.

- **New Moon in Pisces (February 19–March 20):** With both the sun and moon in Pisces at the new moon, it can be a powerful time for peaceful transitions and new beginnings with spiritual endeavors, dreams, relationships, and desire to go with the flow. Use this moon for artistic and creative endeavors as well as to heal old wounds for a fresh start. Furthermore, the spiritual nature of this sign makes this moon a great time for integrating regular meditations for psychic development and plunging into past lives.
- **Full Moon in Pisces (August 23–September 22):** Amid detail-oriented, physical Virgo season, the Pisces full moon invites energies of dreams and spirituality—and balance between the two. You can utilize the Pisces moon to get in touch with your spiritual and creative energies to accompany Virgo productivity. Or you can dream big and use the Virgo sun to add practicality and planning to the mix. For some, the Pisces moon may highlight a need or desire to bring balance not just to the physical body but also to spiritual practices and intuition. As a water sign, Pisces is deeply intuitive, so use this time for psychic dreaming, getting in touch with your intuition, and checking any triggers for healing. You may be extra sensitive at this time, so channel that energy into personal growth and reflection.

Void-of-Course Moon

The void-of-course moon is a time when the moon doesn't appear to be traveling through any particular sign. This is based on the constellations set by Western astrology. The void-of-course moon can present an opportunity to reflect and rest. Some astrologers cite this as a time not to start new things or anything that you wish to see lasting results from. For those who practice magic, this is a time when astrologers would advise not to do spells. However, if you have an important matter to address, you can't forgo it simply because the moon is void of course. So focus on areas of rest where you can, and take it slow in other areas. You can also use this time to reflect on your inner self a bit more freely.

MOON MINERALS AND OTHER CRYSTALS

From ancient royal malachite carvings to magical amulets, crystals have been revered for their magical and energetic properties throughout time. And as the names *moonstone* and *sunstone* might suggest, some of these crystals are believed to draw down the energy of various planets and celestial bodies. Through their energetic and historical associations, the following crystals can help enhance the intentions of your moon magic in Part 2. Refer to Appendix A: Astrological Reference List for information on which crystals are associated with each astrological sign.

Amazonite

A beautiful stone with soothing, light blue-green hues, amazonite helps establish self-awareness and assists with clear communication. A stone of honesty, amazonite will encourage inner harmony while revealing one's personal truth and promoting the confidence and wisdom to live and communicate that truth to the world.

Amber

Amber is a strong stone for creativity, sensuality, and empowerment. It assists with healing, helping to imbue the body with light energy to alleviate depression and anxiety. As a fossilized botanical resin, amber is also great for connecting to ancient wisdom and uncovering deep-rooted energetic patterns.

Amethyst

One of the most popular modern stones for meditation, amethyst connects one to the divine and to spiritual wisdom. It is a great stone for developing intuitive abilities while also providing auric protection. A wonderful stone for stress relief, amethyst helps break addictive patterns and invites peaceful rest.

Ametrine

A combination of two of the most popular stones, ametrine beautifully integrates the potency of wise and intuitive amethyst with positive and creative citrine. Ametrine can help one connect to divine wisdom and invoke spiritual and mental clarity, while also encouraging them to find their own power and overcome fear or self-sabotage.

Aquamarine

Aquamarine is a stone of both calm and courage. Its peaceful and cleansing energy helps clear the mind of phobias and the judgment of others, making way for wisdom, mental clarity, and inner knowing. As its name suggests, it is associated with water, and thus the moon and feminine energy. Aquamarine is therefore often used for healing, learning to go with the flow, and connecting to goddess energy for calm communication. It is also often used for safe travel, spiritual insight, and opening the way for new perspectives and ideas.

Aragonite

Aragonite is a stone of vitality, expression, and balance. In its raw star-cluster form, aragonite helps to disperse energetic blockages and clear the energy body. It can help one attune to wisdom for problem-solving as well as inspire emotional growth and self-healing.

Bismuth

Bismuth embodies the energy of transformation and acts as a conduit for journeying among the physical, spiritual, and astral realms. These associations make bismuth great for shamanic journeying or for visualization. Bismuth promotes energetic support for those who feel overburdened or experience feelings of isolation. It can provide focus and wisdom in times of need.

Black Kyanite

Black kyanite is a great stone for removing negative energy, cutting away toxic ties, and helping to heal tears in the energy body. A darker variation of traditional blue kyanite, this grounding stone also helps with aligning chakras and assists with clairvoyance.

Black Moonstone

In comparison to white and rainbow moonstones, which resemble the full moon, black moonstone bears semblance to the new moon. Therefore, this powerful stone is useful for new beginnings and for inner journeying, grounding, and protection. Black moonstone is a great crystal to work with for in-between energy and finding inner power.

Bloodstone

Bloodstone inspires endurance and vitality with respect to one's goals. While not a lunar crystal, this red-dotted green stone is a great addition for harvest moons as well as moons related to achieving goals, vibrancy, strength, and confidence. Bloodstone inspires courage in the face of obstacles and change. It is also an excellent stone to dispel loneliness and fear.

Blue Lace Agate

With ribbons of varying blue hues, this stone inspires harmony, eases anxiety, promotes support, and releases blockages that prevent self-expression. Its energy is particularly great for keeping the peace and inspiring communication in group dynamics.

Carnelian

Carnelian is believed to invoke courage and boldness. In addition to aiding with these leadership qualities, it helps give physical vitality and vigor and is beneficial for people who are seeking to take that first step or looking for the energy to pursue their dreams.

Emerald

Emerald is a great stone for inspiring one to overcome a scarcity mindset. It assists one in attuning to divine love and feeling safe in expressing compassion toward themselves as they explore their inner worth. It is often associated with wealth, abundance, and wisdom.

Flower Agate

The image and name of flower agate itself may certainly inspire an excitement for the coming spring, and the energetic properties of this stone make it a great crystal ally to work with a fresh start. Flower agate helps to negate stress and restlessness and combat one's own inner fears in favor of inspiring dreams and revelations.

Fluorite

Known as a focusing stone, fluorite helps to clear the mind of debris. In this way, fluorite can soothe anxiety and worry. This is a wonderful stone for students and for focusing intention and productivity!

Garnet

Garnet aids in connection to the energies of survival and draws repressed emotions to the surface for healing. It can help one attune to their instincts and remember what motivates them. Garnet is also a stone of passion, love, and sensuality and will help feed the fire needed to pursue aspirations!

Golden Apatite

Golden apatite, also called yellow apatite, is a golden-colored form of the apatite crystal. It helps instill one with confidence and motivation, replenishing one's sense of self-worth. Golden apatite helps stimulate the metabolism and detoxify energetic blockages that have resulted in repressed emotions and depression. Additionally, it can improve clarity and focus.

Green Aventurine

Green aventurine is a wonderful stone to use for prosperity, bringing in new opportunities, and clearing other people's energy out of your aura and emotional body. It helps one release attachment to outcomes, inviting optimism, joy, good luck, and vitality.

Iolite-Sunstone

With the creative potential of both sunstone and iolite, this crystal is tremendous for communicating and expressing creativity from a spiritual center. It is particularly great at enhancing intuition and communication with one's inner guides. While iolite can help solve problems and keep one calm, the addition of sunstone helps one take inspired action to solve these problems with vitality and confidence. Iolite-sunstone also helps one communicate their truth with confidence.

Kunzite

Kunzite is a high-vibrational stone that connects one to the unconditional love of the universe. This link invites a loving, meditation-like state that produces positive, warm thoughts and actions. By inspiring self-acceptance, this stone can help to center the user and support free self-expression and creativity. Kunzite is also a clearing stone for this reason, helping to remove energy blockages.

Labradorite

Labradorite is excellent for opening psychic abilities. At the same time, it is a protective stone, keeping one's aura intact and guarded from others as one develops their intuitive abilities. It is also a wonderful stone for assistance during times of transition and change.

Lapis Lazuli

Lapis lazuli is a great ally for psychic development and clear communication. This stone can aid in accessing other realms and communicating with guides. Lapis lazuli is a great stone for journeying for this reason, and it can also be used to journey within oneself to uncover and heal karmic cycles.

Lepidolite

Lepidolite promotes serenity and calm. It helps to balance the emotional body, enabling one to remain centered and unaffected in response to challenging situations. As a result, lepidolite is a great stone for people who deal with excessive fear or worry, helping them to live more mindfully in the moment.

Opal

Opal is quite the enchanting stone. Often revealing flashes of various colors and containing trapped water, this crystal helps to inspire dreams and enhance psychic abilities. It can also help one to balance moods and release fear that may be holding them back.

Peach Moonstone
Like all moonstone varieties, peach moonstone assists with intuitive development and emotional balance. But it is also a stone of fertility and sensuality. A particularly soothing stone, it has a loving energy that makes it especially potent for energetically sensitive people.

Pink Chalcedony
Pink chalcedony is a great stone for working with feminine energy and embracing self-love and self-esteem. This crystal particularly helps one work through and understand their fears in order to heal. It also helps to enhance trust of one's intuition.

Rhodochrosite
Rhodochrosite is a powerful stone for emotional healing, self-love, and compassion. This stone helps one reconnect with their inner child, invoking creativity, play, and self-expression. This child-like energy helps one feel more confident in inspiring others to pursue their dreams.

Rose Quartz
One of the most popular go-tos in the modern crystal world, this stone helps one gently connect with universal love, release worry and stress, and invite emotional and spiritual healing. It helps one to see the beauty in themselves and give and receive the love that exists all around.

Ruby
Ruby is a potent heart and love stone. It balances and protects the heart chakra, helping to regulate emotions and stimulate awareness, expression, and passion. Its strong heart connection inspires bliss by connecting the user to the divine love all around. Ruby is also great for success.

Selenite

A crystallized type of gypsum formed in salt, selenite is one of the most popular minerals for energetic purification, protection, and connecting to one's higher self. Named after the moon goddess Selene, selenite is a wonderful choice for connecting to higher, cosmic vibrations.

Turquoise

Turquoise is a stone sacred for its association with the divine and creation. As many blue stones do, turquoise helps promote communication. However, it also helps one embrace self-forgiveness and acceptance in order to find healing and wisdom.

EDIBLE ELEMENTS

When creating lunar cocktails, the herbs, fruits, and other flavors you use play very important roles in the potency of the drinks as well as the specific energies captured within them. In this section, you will learn about the edible elements you will use to mix the aligned lunar libations in Part 2. Some of these ingredients are used in the liqueurs, bitters, infused drinking vinegars (called "shrubs"), and infusions stirred into different cocktails. Others will be added directly to the drinks for fresh, flavorful combinations inspired by the various moons! Refer back to the Astrological Signs and the Moon section in this chapter for more information on the planets and elements linked to different ingredients.

Agave

Also known as maguey, agave is a relative of the asparagus plant. It blooms once every 10–25 years and must be quickly harvested before its death in order to make tequila and mezcal. It is associated with the planet Mars and the element of fire and thus is great for love and sex/lust workings. Given its interesting life cycle, it is also great for coming into one's power, beauty, and reflections on life and death.

Allspice

Containing the flavors of many favorite spices, such as pepper, cinnamon, clove, and nutmeg, allspice packs a punch in both flavor and energy. Allspice is often use magically for attraction, money, luck, healing, creativity, and power. In mixology, allspice can be added through ground spice, or through an allspice/pimento dram such as St. Elizabeth.

Almond

An essential in various cooking and baking ingredients and treats, almond has beguiled and enchanted humankind throughout time. Beyond their uses in food and cooking, almonds have often been utilized magically for abundance and money as well as to impart wisdom and help to invoke success. Given as wedding favors, almonds are also often seen as symbols of love, and can help promote compassion. Sweet almonds are the nontoxic variety that people eat, while bitter almonds may be used in processing foods once the toxins are removed. Almond is associated with Mercury and the element of air. Amaretto, an almond-flavored liqueur, is sometimes not made from almond at all, but from the pits of apricots, which almond is actually related to.

Aloe Vera

Familiar to many for its use in first aid, aloe vera is indeed magically used to soothe and heal. However, this plant is also used for protection as well as luck. It is associated with the moon, Jupiter, Venus, and the element of water. Surprisingly, aloe vera has one of the most bitter flavors because of a component called aloin. It is for this reason that aloe is sometimes employed in bitter amari such as fernet.

Anise

Anise has a strong purification essence and is particularly potent when used with bay leaves. It is great for protection, divination, connecting to spirits, and youth. It is associated with the planet Jupiter and the element of air.

Apple

From sayings like "an apple a day keeps the doctor away," it's easy to guess that apple is associated with health, healing, and longevity. Apples have been around for millions of years, with each apple having its own unique DNA. With this ancestry, apples are often used for accessing ancient wisdom and honoring life cycles, especially around the harvest season, when the fruit is especially celebrated for abundance. Associated with Venus, apples have also been used to bring in love, as well as aid in love divination. All the magic held in this fruit can be seen through the five-pointed star representing wisdom, manifestation, and a portal to the divine.

Apricot

This delicious fruit is a go-to for inspiring love and gaining the favor of others. As one might guess from these connections, it is associated with Venus and the element of water.

Banana

While little is known of the banana's origins, it was sacred to many cultures. Just as every part of this plant is usable, bananas have many magical associations ranging from abundance and creativity to love and money. Banana is associated with Mars, Venus, and the elements of air and water.

Barley

Originating in the fertile crescent of the Middle East, barley quickly became a staple grain sacred to deities in ancient Egypt, India, Sumeria, and Greece. Barley is associated with Venus and the element of earth, hinting at its magical capabilities of fertility, love, and abundance. It is also often used for healing and dispersing negativity.

Basil

Basil is a great heart-opening herb. It has a strong association with love and was once used as a token of affection. Its potent aroma associates it with protection as it cleanses the air and invokes clarity and wisdom for decision-making. Basil also calms the nerves and helps bring in harmony and prosperity.

Bay Leaf

The bay leaf is a multidimensional magical herb, providing enhancement to one's psychic powers and prophetic dreams while also offering protection from negativity. It is also used for wisdom and is well known for the wishing ritual of writing down one's wish on a bay leaf and then burning it to manifest the wish.

Beet

This red root vegetable has been used to promote beauty as well as longevity, and with its enchanting red hue, it's also a go-to for inspiring love. Beet is associated with Saturn as well as the element of earth.

Bergamot

Bergamot is a bitter citrus well known for flavoring Earl Grey tea. It is used to promote meditation, calm, a positive disposition, and mental clarity for decision-making. Like many citruses, bergamot is helpful for boosting joy in one's life and inspiring inner strength. However, bergamot in particular is used to cultivate success and personal power. Bergamot is connected to the planet Mercury and the element of air as well as the moon and the planet Venus, making it a powerful go-to.

Blackberry

Another potent lunar ingredient, blackberry (also known as bramble) is a luscious, sensual berry. While the thorns of the blackberry bush are thought to be protective, the plant as a whole is associated with healing and is often used to pay homage to the Irish goddess Brigid. Given its seasonal bounty, blackberry has strong associations with the harvest and is celebrated at various harvest festivals to draw in abundance and money. In folklore, bramble is thought to be particularly connected to magic and fairies and thus can help increase one's connection to the natural realm. Blackberry is also deeply grounding and can be eaten to increase sexual desire. Blackberry is connected to the moon, Venus, and the element of water.

Black Peppercorn

A popular cooking herb in everything from your breakfast scrambled eggs to your evening soup, black peppercorn has a long history of use. Used medicinally in Greece as early as 500 B.C.E., and used in cooking for more than four thousand years, it is added to protective foods and used in purification diets. It is often used for protection against the evil eye, to cleanse the mind, and to dispel evil.

Blueberry

The blueberry is another delicious berry associated with the moon and the element of water. A treat packed with antioxidants and various other nutrients that help protect the body, blueberries are magically associated with protection. In fact, they are particularly used for psychic and magical protection, which only furthers their ability to help induce peace and calm.

Butterfly Pea Flower

Popular in Southeast Asia, butterfly pea flower is a magical flower from pea plants. When steeped in water, it offers a beautifully blue color that changes to purple when mixed with acid like lemon juice. Generally, peas are associated with Venus and the elements of earth and water, promoting love, abundance, and money. However, the pea flower adds in energies of transformation, happiness, and spirituality.

Cacao

Responsible for one of the most beloved treats on earth (chocolate), cacao comes from a tropical evergreen that grows along the equator. Associated with Mars and the element of fire, cacao—especially in the form of chocolate—is connected with love. It has been considered a food of the gods and also helps invoke prosperity and abundance. It can also uplift one's mood and improve concentration.

Cardamom

Often added to apple pies and wine to help inspire love and lust, this expensive spice actually has compounds that reduce stress. It is associated with Venus and the element of water.

Celery

Now a symbol of healthy eating, celery was once eaten by Roman women to encourage lust—perhaps due to its association with the element of fire. This herbaceous ingredient is also associated with the planet Mercury, helping to enhance concentration, psychic awareness, and overall health.

Cherry

With over 120 varieties of cherry trees, this fruit is a key love and happiness ingredient. True to its Venus association, the cherry blossom is often used to stimulate and attract romance or to bless a marriage for fertility and happiness. This fruit is used for abundance, to attract good luck and optimism, and to help one see past obstacles. Beyond its use in love magic, cherry juice is also used to represent blood. Cherry is also associated with Mercury and the elements of water and fire.

Cinnamon

From candles to scented brooms decorating the home, cinnamon has become a marker of the shift of seasons to fall and winter. Fittingly, it is thus used for protection in the home. Cinnamon is a powerful spice that raises the vibrations of all things, making it great for spirituality and situations in which one needs fast luck, such as manifesting money or abundance. An attractant, it is used for enhancing personal power and also adding a bit of zest to love and sex magic. For special money mixes, the gold flake cinnamon liqueur, Goldschlager, is always a great choice!

Clove

This warming spice is associated with Jupiter and the element of fire. It is often burned to attract money, cleanse negativity and gossip, and purify and raise the spiritual energies of a place. It also helps to bring in love and is a fast favorite for comfort during the winter months.

Coconut

With its round shape and white milk, it is of little surprise that this nutritious and soothing food is associated with the moon and the element of water. In fact, coconut is linked to the Hawaiian moon goddess Hina, and has been used as an offering throughout the Pacific and in some practices of the Afro-Caribbean diaspora. Coconut is seen as sacred and is also used for inner purification and enhancing psychic awareness. The hard shell of coconut can symbolize home protection.

Coffee

The "beans" from which coffee is brewed are actually seeds that grow in pairs in the small red fruit of a shrub thought to have originated in Ethiopia. Caffeine gives coffee energy-induced associations related to Mars and the element of fire. Caffeine actually has many uses in folk magic, as a form of divination and for cleansing and clarity magic. It is popular in many liqueurs and alcoholic drinks like the Irish coffee.

Cranberry

A fall favorite, this bright berry is associated with protection, and eaten for such. However, due to its red color, cranberry is sometimes also used for love and abundance. Ruled by action-oriented Mars, cranberry can be useful for following through with goals and passion.

Cucumber

Associated with beauty, youth, and healing, cucumber is a refreshing and easy go-to for moon beauty mixes. It can also assist in matters of peace and stress relief. Plentiful with seeds, cucumber is also great for fertility of all kinds.

Dill

Few scents match the strength of dill, a common kitchen herb from the Mediterranean. Dill is commonly displayed or used in various areas of the home for protection, good luck, and even peaceful rest. Abundant with seeds, dill's display of plenty makes it a go-to for calling in money and abundance. As one might expect of an ingredient associated with Mercury and the element of air, dill also helps to clear and stimulate the mind, improve focus, and even enhance creativity. Dill is often thought to help protect against evil and negativity, and to fortify one's spirit for success. Its association with love and lust helps to release any hexes toward love, as well as balance lust.

Egg

A symbol of birth and life, it's of little surprise that the egg is such a sacred image in many cultures across the globe. It is often employed in healing to help cleanse or used in divination. Its shell is a symbol of protection and purification. In cocktails, egg can also give texture and mellow out harsh flavors.

Elder

Popular for both its berries and its flowers, elder has a long history of use stemming back to the Stone Age. It is often used to connect to nature spirits such as fairies, and is thought to assist with healing and strengthening one's power. Additionally, elder is useful for prosperity and good fortune, while also helping to protect and cleanse away any negative energy. This enchanting ingredient is associated with both Venus and Mercury, as well as all the natural elements.

Ginger

Associated with Mars and the element of fire, it's no surprise ginger is used to stimulate energy, especially for love and lust. The strength and power of this incredible spice is also used to promote success, power, and money, and to guarantee the successfulness of spells. And it certainly has its uses in healing magic and physicality.

Grape

Sacred to many deities, such as Dionysus of the ancient Greeks, grape and its products are associated with spiritual communication and communion. The decadence of this fruit has also tied grape to magical themes of abundance and money. Growing together in bunches, grapes are used to help influence fertility. When eaten, grape is believed to help produce dreams as well as strengthen the mind. Grape is connected to the moon and the element of water.

Grapefruit

A hybrid between the sweet orange and pomelo, grapefruit is thought to have originated in Barbados in the seventeenth century. Associated with the sun, the moon, and the element of water, grapefruit is great for purification and positivity. It has become a favorite for mixers in drinks like the Salty Dog and Paloma.

Hazelnut

Hazelnut is associated with wisdom and divination. It is used to aid in various magics, and its associations with the sun and Mercury make it a great ingredient to use for creative ideas. It is also excellent for protection.

Hibiscus

Hibiscus, whether as a tea or a flower, has long been used for love and lust workings. And with its seductive red-magenta color and associations with Venus and the element of water, this is no surprise. In some magical traditions, hibiscus is also used to aid divination.

Honey

One of the first sweeteners in the world, honey is a great source for healing and wisdom. The product of bees, it also represents hard work and abundance. Seen as sacred to many deities, honey is also associated with fertility and sensuality. Honey is linked to the sun and the element of air.

Jasmine

With a fragrance as bewitching as the moon, jasmine is often used to attract love and to invoke a sense of mental peace, calm, and clarity. Beyond its floral appeal, jasmine is a highly spiritual herb, often used for spirit communication, enhancing intuition, and dream work. Its magical ability to help one connect to spiritual sources also makes it great for inspiring new ideas and creativity. Additionally, this potent flower is known in many magical communities for bringing abundance and attracting luck in one's fortune. Jasmine is associated with Mercury, the moon, and the elements of air, earth, and water.

Lavender

Few scents are as calming and soothing as lavender. It is often used in essential oil form and in sachet bags to help induce tranquility and reduce stress. Lavender's association with Mercury and the element of air, along with its ability to invoke peace, make it a go-to for communication and harmony in any relationship. Soothing away negativity, lavender can help in matters of purification and peaceful rest. Its ability to induce calm and release stress makes it particularly useful for lifting one's mood, promoting longevity, and inviting healing into one's life. Additionally, lavender has also been used to attract love and promote fidelity in relationships.

Lemon

Lemon is an essential in a number of cocktails and beverages and is directly associated with the moon. In fact, many scientists refer to the nodules on either side of the lemon as an example of the shape of the moon. Lemon is used for purification and cleansing in magic. Nostalgic lemon-focused foods like pies and custards mirror lemon's capacity for inspiring joy and fidelity in love and relationships of all kinds. This vibrant fruit is also thought to boost energy and mood! Lemon is connected to the element of water.

Lemon Balm

A member of the mint family, lemon balm is a powerful healing herb associated with the moon and the element of water. This herb is often used magically to help with success and healing, but it is also often taken to assist with pain and a variety of other ailments. Like many mint family members, lemon balm helps relieve stress and invoke a sense of peace and rejuvenation, thereby aiding mental faculties and cognitive function. It is commonly used for cleansing and purifying purposes and is particularly helpful for cleansing away bad luck in love (and thus attracting a new lover).

Lime

Lime is another key citrus ingredient in craft cocktails, and similarly to lemon, it is used for love and purification. However, lime is associated with the sun and the element of fire, and it is tied to various healing magics and can be used for cleansing away hexes and protection from the evil eye.

Maple

The leaves of maple have uses in love spells and rituals, and the syrup is thought to be a love stimulant. Ruled by Jupiter, maple is often used for longevity and money, and it is believed that the branches of maple trees may have once served as magical wands. With its grounding flavors, maple is associated with the elements of air and earth.

Melon

A summertime favorite, melon is enjoyed through both honeydew and cantaloupe. Believed to be native to India and Africa, melon has long been used in healing and purification practices. Melon is associated with the moon and the element of water, and has also been used to induce love and abundance.

Milk

From your morning milk to your coffee creamer, milk of all kinds plays a central role in the kitchen. This nurturing ingredient is associated with the moon and the element of water. Having a history of use in deity offerings and being associated with powerful goddesses such as Hathor, milk is also great for connecting to goddess energies, for fertility and beauty workings. It also helps one open up to love.

Mint

As its refreshing flavor and aroma might hint, mint is associated with the mind and memory. Spearmint is associated with Venus and can add extra layers of love, whereas peppermint is associated with Mercury and can have extra potency for communication and thought. Both are associated with abundance, protection, purification, and psychic abilities.

Nutmeg

In the era of the spice trade, nutmeg became renowned and could bring a lot of wealth to those who sold it, so it's no wonder this spice is associated with money magic as well as luck. Nutmeg has also long been considered healing, and modern science shows it can help with issues regarding digestion, depression, sleep, and more. This spice can also be used to increase psychic awareness, ensure fidelity, and influence one's mood to be more positive. Nutmeg is associated with Jupiter, the moon, and the element of fire.

Oak

Oak is intimately tied to the history of mankind as an early source of sustenance. As such, oak is seen as an elder in the plant kingdom and used to connect to ancient and ancestral knowledge. Oak is often regarded as a source of magical protection, even from lightning, harm, and illness. It is ruled by both the sun and Jupiter, making it a superb choice for luck and strength. Oak is also believed to aid in cleansing as well as fertility. In the world of cocktails, oak has a unique pliability and strength that make it a go-to for transporting and flavoring spirits.

Oat

Like other grains, oat is associated with money and prosperity. However, perhaps due to its use for nutrition or in comforting cakes and warm foods, it has a particularly nurturing association. Oat is associated with Venus and the element of earth.

Olive

It's called "offering an olive branch" for a reason: Olive is associated with peace and luck. It is also associated with spirituality and is tied to various religious practices. Olive is also associated with help, healing, fertility, and lust. The branches are also used for protection from evil and lightning. Olive is associated with the sun and the elements of fire and air.

Orange

From the use of its blossoms in perfume for beauty and attraction to the use of its peels in tea or juices in morning breakfast rituals, orange is an essential ingredient. In folk and magical practices, orange is associated with love, luck, prosperity, happiness, and purification. Its associations with the sun and the element of fire also help inspire creativity and attraction.

Papaya

Believed to be native to Central America, papaya has been and still is used as an aphrodisiac. This enticing tropical fruit is thus associated with love and lust. Packed with digestive enzymes, papaya is often integrated into wellness and beauty practices, making this moon- and water-associated ingredient perfect for lunar workings for beauty and youth.

Passion Fruit

Popular in tropical drinks, both alcoholic and nonalcoholic alike, this moon- and water-associated ingredient invites love and passion (as the name might suggest). This delightful fruit is believed to be native to Brazil and is also associated with peace.

Peach

Sacred to some Chinese traditions, the peach is associated with longevity and wisdom; everything from the tree itself to the flowers, fruits, and seeds is used for religious purposes. Magically, peach is used for health, purification, and especially love. Associated with Venus and the element of water, the peach is said to help one expand their ability to give and receive love.

Pear

With its trees sometimes bearing fruit for as long as three hundred years, the pear is associated with longevity. Besides this healing association, pear is often used in love and lust spells to increase attraction. It can also be used to bring in abundance and money. Pear is linked to Venus, the moon, and the element of water.

Pineapple

It's hard not to feel happy while enjoying some vibrant, zesty pineapple! Once used as a symbol of hospitality, it is associated with kindness and happiness. Pineapple is also often used for prosperity, money, and healing, as well as protection and inducing love. Associated with the sun and the element of fire, pineapple can also be great for inspiring a positive disposition or creativity.

Pomegranate

The magic of the pomegranate extends deep into human history. Oftentimes, the red color of the fruit is perceived as the blood of life, with the accompanying bountiful seeds representing creative potential and fertility. Pomegranate is sacred to the goddess Persephone and is often used during Samhain practices to honor the dead and revitalize the spirit through the winter months. It is believed to be protective and also great for increase. Pomegranate is associated with the planet Mercury and the element of fire.

Poppy

Associated with the moon and the element of water, poppy is often used in mixtures to help with sleep and to find answers in one's dreams. It is also used to induce love, as well as fertility, luck, and money.

Pumpkin

Often combined with lunar-associated nutmeg, pumpkin is a delicious go-to for abundance moon magic. As the modern practice of carving pumpkins for Halloween may indicate, this harvest vegetable has associations with witchcraft. When combined with spices like nutmeg and clove, it becomes a powerhouse for attraction and prosperity of all kinds. Pumpkin is associated with mother goddesses, the moon, and the element of earth, and is also believed to be healing. Pumpkin seeds can be used for divination.

Raspberry

It should come as no surprise that this delightful red berry is believed to help induce happiness and love. Associated with Venus and the element of water, raspberry is often eaten to inspire joy and loving feelings.

Rhubarb

A tart, bright red stalk, rhubarb has made its name in pies and crumbles and is now making its way to mixology as a unique bitter ingredient. It is associated with Venus and the element of earth, and thus is often used for love as well as fidelity in relationships. Native to China, rhubarb is used in Eastern herbalism and is also associated with protection.

Rice

Typically used in cocktails through sake, rice is often believed to protect against negative energy and is dispersed around the home for protection and good luck. Once a source of currency in feudal Japan, rice is also a symbol of prosperity and fertility. In China as well as Western tradition, rice is thrown at newlywed couples for good fortune, fertility, and happiness. Rice is associated with the sun and the element of air.

Rose

Few scents are as evocative and enchanting as rose. And while it is one of the key associations for love and beauty magic, its energetic potential extends far beyond that! Rose also has powerful healing energies and can be burned along with rosemary and other cleansing herbs to purify a room before a healing session. Additionally, it helps to promote soothing, positive vibes, dispelling negative energy. Its thorns are wonderful for protection and boundary magic. Rose is also great as a tea to enhance psychic abilities before divination or rest. In magical mixology, rose is used through liqueurs, rose water, and syrups. It is associated with Venus, the moon, and the element of earth.

Rosemary

Rosemary is a powerful cleansing herb, often burned to dispel negativity or to clear space before ritual and magic. This cleansing capacity helps invoke peace that is useful for restful sleep but can also enhance one's psychic abilities. Associated with knowledge retention and memory, rosemary can help enhance cognition as well. Rosemary is linked to Mercury, the sun, the moon, and the element of fire.

Rye

Rye is a common ingredient in various beers and whiskeys. Magically, rye has associations with love and fidelity, as it can survive in the coldest of climates. It is affiliated with Venus and the element of earth.

Saffron

Saffron is famous as an expensive and powerful spice. It is often used for strength and happiness but can also be employed for love, healing, and psychic power. As its bright orange hue might suggest, it is associated with the sun and the element of fire.

Sage

Popular in both cooking and folk traditions around the world, culinary sage has many uses in mixology. In folk practices, it is often used for purification and psychic protection. Associated with Mercury, it is great for improving focus, clairvoyance, and communication with both the spirit and with others. As its association with Jupiter might suggest, sage is also used in magical matters of wisdom and longevity, and even to grant wishes.

Salt

From salt mines buried deep in the earth, it's not much of a leap to see that salt is associated with both the planet earth and the element of earth. Countless traditions around the world recognize salt as purifying and protective. It can help one energetically ground in order to feel more connected to the earth, or help ground intentions for manifestation. It's often used as an energetic cleanser for psychic protection as well.

Strawberry

Popular as a chocolate-covered Valentine's Day sweet, this delectable red berry is indeed associated with love, the planet Venus, and the element of water. In magic, strawberry is used to help stimulate love interest as well as enhance love divination. A berry that inspires happiness with its very flavor, this ingredient is great for manifesting harmony and good luck.

Sugarcane

Due to its sweetening nature, sugarcane is an attractant, used to sweeten people up to others and draw in love. In many cultural traditions, sugar is left as an offering, and its love energy can help dispel negativity. In magical mixology, the power of sugarcane is invoked most directly through rum and syrups but also through anything that has cane sugar added.

Thyme

A culinary, garden, and witch favorite, thyme is a multipurpose herb that is used for everything from good health to purification and psychic abilities. It is also used to inspire courage and love. Associated with Venus and the element of water, thyme is especially powerful when burned before healing work or in healing spells, and it is great for peaceful sleep and dreams.

Tomato

Little stirs memories like the summer tomato harvest. As a harvest ingredient, it is no surprise that it is often used for money and prosperity. Its bright red color reminds one of its association with the planet Venus, and its juiciness the element of the water, making it no surprise that its seeds are sometime used for attracting love. It is also associated with protection for keeping evil from the home and is representative of health.

Turmeric

Turmeric is a powerful spice. In India, it is burned to cleanse demons, while in Hawaii it is often used for purification. Turmeric can help boost one's mood in addition to detoxifying their energy. It is also used for creativity and helps enhance the mind and memory, which should come as little surprise due to its association with Mercury and the element of air.

Vanilla

Often used in magic to encourage love (especially when combined with sugar), vanilla can help sweeten dispositions and invoke peace and happiness. As an attractant, it is often used for inducing lust, but it can also be great for money, manifestation, luck, and attracting magic of all kinds. The cured fruit of an orchid, this unique and enchanting spice is also associated with restoring energy and helping inspire better mental faculty. Vanilla is linked to Venus and the element of water.

Vinegar

Vinegar is essentially any acidic liquid. Thus, it can be made from many ingredients. In some witchcraft practices, vinegar is used for purification and protection. Generally, it is associated with Saturn and the element of fire.

Violet

Violet's romantic association extends beyond mere children's poems: it is indeed often used to promote love, especially when combined with lavender. Among the first flowers to greet the spring, at times even blooming amid the snow, violets are connected to hope and happiness. Just like they can signal the turning of the season toward spring, they are believed to bring a turn of one's luck. A common scent for bed linens, this enchanting bloom is also associated with dream work as well as peace and breaking evil spells. Violet is linked to Venus and the elements of water and air.

Walnut

In European folk medicine, walnut was used to treat problems of the brain, perhaps due to its brain-like shape. Thus, it is of little surprise that this ingredient is used in magic to stimulate the mind. With its hard shell, it is also used for strength and protection. Additionally, it is thought to be helpful in granting wishes. It is associated with the sun and the element of fire.

Watermelon

Native to Africa, watermelon is associated with the moon and used in healing and fertility rituals. Watermelon flavors make great vodka, tequila, and rum concoctions and can be infused into cocktails through fresh watermelon, watermelon juice, and watermelon liqueurs.

Wheat

Used in everything from beer to vodka and whiskey, wheat is a crucial ingredient. But beyond the spirits industry, wheat also has many traditions in cultures all over the world. Associated with both the planet Venus and the element of earth, wheat is often used for fertility, abundance, and prosperity workings to draw in riches and money. It is regarded as a symbol of the harvest and of fruitfulness of all kinds. Beyond this, like other grains, wheat also holds the seeds of the future, representing the past, present, and potential of the future all in one.

Wormwood

Wormwood's use in spirits and alcohol dates as far back as ancient Egypt and China, where it was often infused into medicinal wines to treat stomach maladies and round-worms. It is found in some vermouths, French and Italian liqueurs, and more popularly in absinthe. Magically, wormwood is often burned to enhance psychic abilities, and is also used for protection against spells as well as to summon spirits. Absinthe in particular is used for love mixtures. It is particularly great for working with the moon. Wormwood is associated with Mars and the element of fire.

DRAWING DOWN THE MOON

Before you dig in to the delicious lunar libations in Part 2, it is important to understand how to energetically work with the moon—to call it down for its power. In the following sections, you will learn some basic techniques to help you tune in to the moon, set intentions for potent moon magic, and develop a closer relationship with the moon.

Mirroring the Moon

The first step to tuning in to the moon and using its energies in your magical workings is to look up what phase and sign the moon is in. Revisit the sections on moon phases and astrological signs earlier in this chapter for a refresher on what themes the moon in this phase and sign present. Then spend some time writing about what's going on in your life: What needs healing or perhaps even changing in these areas?

Once you know what sign and phase the moon is in and what you wish to manifest or alter in your life, you can choose a beverage by energetic alignment, or by referencing Appendix A: Astrological Reference List for the cocktail associated with each moon sign. Then you can either start crafting your beverage, or meditate to set the tone before mixing the chosen drink.

Meditating with the Moon

Meditating can be a powerful way to create space for moon magic so that you can hear its wisdom clearly and use it as a guide in your rituals or spells. The first step of meditation is to ground and center your energy. Centering is the act of calling your energy back to your body and the center of your unique experience and perspective on life. There are many ways to do this, but a common method is to use a breathing pattern such as the four-fold breath technique: Breathe in for four seconds, hold the breath for four seconds, then exhale for four seconds. At the very least, focus on taking slow and deep breaths, allowing the breath to expand your stomach. Notice the tightening in your chest with the expansion of air and then the release and relaxation of your shoulders as you exhale. Regardless of the breathing technique you use, focus on how these breaths make you feel, tuning in to your body with each inhale and exhale. You may wish to wave a selenite wand through your aura or take a purifying lunar bath to help facilitate this process.

Once your energy and focus are centered back in your body, it is time to connect with the earth by grounding your energy. Grounding can be as simple as tuning in to the bottoms of your feet as they stand upon the ground, or the places where your legs meet the floor if you are sitting or lying down. Be conscious of the earth's gravitational pull on your body. Some may visualize a single or double cord, or even tree-like roots, extending from their feet or lower abdomen, deep into the earth's core.

Now that you are centered and grounded, it's time to "call down" and connect with the moon. Take a moment to reflect on the energies of the moon, the world, and what is occurring in your life. Perhaps light some incense, such as jasmine, rose, or lemon balm. Close your eyes, take a few deep breaths, and visualize the moon's light shining down on you, slowly illuminating your body from the inside out. Use each inhale to imagine this lunar light growing stronger and brighter within your body, until you feel and envision your entire body aglow.

You can stay here in this visualization, or go a step further in the meditation and visualize a lunar stairway appearing before your feet, stretching all the way to the moon. Travel up the stairs, noting each step and feeling lighter and more luminescent with each one until finally you see yourself before the moon. You may envision a lunar spirit, embodied in an image, an animal, light, or a moon goddess, or you may envisage the astrological sign the moon is in. In this space, you can ask questions of the moon or meditate on its power.

When you feel you have gotten all the guidance or information you need, visualize returning back to your body. See yourself glowing with lunar light, feeling transformed and radiant. Take a few more deep breaths, tuning in to each part of your body, then the earth.

Setting Intentions with the Moon

Once you have completed a moon meditation, you can create your aligned lunar libation and use it to amplify your intentions for magic. You can follow the More Moon Magic activities provided in Part 2 for the cocktail you chose, or mix and match activities and libations.

MAKING YOUR FIRST COSMIC COCKTAIL

As you strengthen your skills in moon mixology, you may feel called to change ingredients. Magic is as unique as one's taste preferences, so always make ingredients work for you, whether in regard to flavor or spiritual preference, budget, or accessibility. Use the recipes in Part 2 as a template, and switch out ingredients as both the moon and your personal desires guide you to.

CHAPTER 4

MAGICAL MOON INGREDIENTS

Centuries ago, a folk healer would harvest ingredients and craft a healing, magical concoction with various herbs and water. And an alchemist would preserve the power of rosemary and other natural ingredients in alcohol to use their energies in future months or even years. In fact, many foundational elements that have constructed the modern craft cocktail—shrubs, bitters, infusions, liqueurs, syrups—have ties to ancient practices.

In this chapter, you will find moon-associated recipes blended with potent flavors to further enchant your celestial drinks. From Lunar Limoncello to Moon Drop Bitters, there are magical syrups, infusions, and more to help you craft the magical mixes in Part 2. But don't stop there: Let these recipes inspire you to stir up your own powerful libations under the guiding light of the moon.

MOON WATER ICE CUBES

While they may not be the first thing you think of when you consider concocting a beverage, ice cubes in nonalcoholic and alcoholic drinks alike play a huge roll in the quality—and potentially the moon magic—of your beverage. Whether your drink is shaken, stirred, or on the rocks, the use (or intentional exclusion) of ice lends to the purity, flavor, and energy of a recipe. So why not enhance an average bourbon on the rocks, a Cosmic Wisdom Appletini, or even your favorite nonalcoholic spritzer with some magically charged ice cubes? To make them, simply add a handful of rose petals to a medium bowl. Pour water over them and set the bowl outside at dawn in the sunlight. At noon, remove the infusion from sunlight and strain the rose petals from the water. Fill an ice cube tray halfway with the water, top each cavity with 1 rose petal, and freeze. A few hours later, once frozen, fill the rest of each cavity with water and freeze again.

LUNAR SYRUPS

A key element in craft beverages, syrups can add depth and sweetness to a drink. But in magical mixology, syrups take on another dimension, as a means to layer in additional moon and herbal magic. In particular, various syrup flavors with astrological associations can be used to call down certain signs or zodiac energies intended for a cocktail.

Selecting a Syrup Sweetener

Looking to charm a love interest? Hoping to get into the good graces of your boss? In magic workings, sugar is a notorious way to "sweeten" people up. Beyond that, each type of sugar offers a unique flavor and properties that, when blended into a syrup, can take your enchanted drinks to the next level.

Sugar

Granulated sugar is one of the most common sweeteners in mixology. Once an expensive ingredient, sugar is associated with money, and its sweetening qualities make it an easy addition to enticing moon magic and lunar love. In mixology, sugar is most often incorporated through Simple Syrup, which is created by combining equal parts sugar and hot water. This helps the sugar blend better in craft concoctions, and it establishes consistency from one cocktail to the next.

Beyond granulated sugar, modern technology has allowed for countless other sugars in mixology, from beet to coconut. In general, all sugars have an energy of attraction, but you can look up the root ingredients of a particular sugar to find out about its potential energetic potency.

Honey

Honey is the sweetener of choice for classic cocktails like the Bee's Knees and Penicillin—as well as a must in honey lemonade! As one of the first sweeteners in the world and the product of bees, honey has a myriad of magical uses, from healing and purification to happiness and wisdom. In mixology, honey is often used through Honey Syrup (see recipe in this chapter).

Agave

A common sweetener for tequila- and mezcal-based drinks, agave syrup can add a subtle nectar-like sweetness, as well as some revitalizing, beautifying, and youthful energy, to your moon mixes.

Maple

While not quite as common in cocktails as some other sweeteners, pure and organic maple syrup is steadily growing in popularity as an innovative way to add hidden depth and dimension to craft beverages. In moon magic, it also adds extra energies of longevity, love, and abundance. Maple can be particularly useful for calling down the Libra and Taurus moons.

Creating Your Celestial Syrup

Once you have your sweetener selected, you are ready to make a syrup! For sugars and honey, you will typically use a one-to-one ratio of sweetener to water to make your syrup. Agave and maple syrups do not need to be cut with water before using in drinks. Your magical syrups also don't have to be used just for moon cocktails! They can be mixed into magical mocktails, iced teas, coffees, and more. Additionally, you can use them to add a layer of hidden flavor to shrubs and liqueurs (see sections later in this chapter). The following syrup recipes are used to craft the drinks in Part 2.

SIMPLE SYRUP

This brew really lives up to its namesake of "simple," and once you learn how to make it, it will have you creating all sorts of innovative syrup variations for your concoctions. From classics like the old-fashioned to fast favorites like the lemon drop martini, countless cocktails rely on Simple Syrup.

Yields 3/4 cup

1/2 cup granulated sugar
1/2 cup hot water

Add sugar to a small, heatproof glass jar or sealable bowl. Pray over it for whatever energy you are going for. Pour hot water into jar and let cool about 10 minutes. Stir. If in a jar, once syrup has cooled a bit, you can place a lid on top and shake it to help it mix better. Place covered jar or bowl in refrigerator until ready to use, up to 1 month.

HONEY SYRUP

Used in classics like the Bee's Knees, Honey Syrup is a great way to introduce the sweetness of flower nectar into your cocktails. Honey Syrup can be great to use for healing concoctions or lunar beverages aligned to the sun during eclipses or at the time of the new moon.

Yields $^7/_8$ cup

1/2 cup water
1/2 cup amber honey

1. Boil water in a small pot over high heat. While you are waiting for water to boil, place honey in a small, heatproof glass jar. Pray over the ingredients as you wait.

2. Pour boiling water into jar. Stir, let cool 10 minutes, strain out herbs (if you used any), then cover and store syrup in refrigerator until ready to use, up to 1 month.

GRENADINE

Grenadine is a popular bar syrup used in cocktails like the tequila sunrise, and nonalcoholic favorites like the Shirley Temple. It has a deep red color and tart flavor that make it a go-to in mixology. Traditionally, Grenadine is made from pomegranate juice, although it can be made with other ingredients, such as black currant juice, that offer similar flavor profiles of sweetness and tartness. Pomegranate is used here for its magical properties of creativity, money, death, fertility, luck, wishes, and wealth.

Yields 1 cup

1 cup pomegranate juice
1/4 cup granulated sugar
2 threads saffron
1 teaspoon orange blossom water

1. Heat pomegranate juice and sugar in a small pot over medium heat. Stir continuously until sugar is dissolved, then add saffron.

2. Once mixture reaches a slight boil, remove pan from heat and let cool, about 10 minutes. Stir in orange blossom water. Pour syrup into a small jar, cover, and store in refrigerator until ready to use, up to 3 weeks.

LEMON BALM GINGER SYRUP

Summon down the moon for your lunar-manifestation needs with this Lemon Balm Ginger Syrup. Utilizing the success-oriented associations of both lemon balm and ginger, this gently minted and spiced syrup is great for celestial workings of new beginnings, power, and healing. You can use lemon balm tea if you don't have dried lemon balm.

Yields $3/4$ cup

$1/2$ cup water
$1/2$ tablespoon dried lemon balm
1 tablespoon peeled and finely chopped ginger
$1/2$ cup granulated sugar

1. Boil water in a small pot over high heat. While waiting for water to boil, place lemon balm and ginger in a small, heatproof bowl or jar, enjoying their restorative fragrances.

2. Pour boiling water over lemon balm and ginger and allow to steep 5 minutes. Stir in sugar, then allow to cool 10 minutes. Once cooled, strain out solids, cover, and store in refrigerator until ready to use, up to 1 month. (You can also refrigerate with solids and strain right before use.)

LUNAR
TRANSFORMATION SYRUP

Embrace the transformative power of the moon in any lunar mix with this captivating syrup. Using the color-changing magic of butterfly pea flower and the soothing energies of lavender and vanilla, this tasty syrup will turn from blue/indigo to magenta/purple when it comes into contact with acid. Use in lunar libations for change, transformation, and inspiring peace.

Yields 3/4 cup

1/2 cup water
1 (1") piece vanilla bean
1 tablespoon dried butterfly pea flower
1/2 tablespoon dried lavender flowers
1/2 cup sugar

1. Boil water in a small pot over high heat. While waiting for water to boil, use a paring knife to split vanilla bean lengthwise to expose seeds inside, then place in a small, heatproof glass jar with butterfly pea flower and lavender. Pour boiling water over ingredients and allow to steep 5 minutes.

2. Stir in sugar, then allow to cool 10 minutes. Strain out solids immediately after cooling, or allow to sit in refrigerator up to 24 hours to allow butterfly pea flower to infuse properly before straining. Once solids are strained out, syrup can be stored up to 1 month in refrigerator.

Lunar Transformation
Syrup

Rose, Jasmine, and
Rosemary Syrup

Lemon Balm Ginger Syrup

ROSE, JASMINE, AND ROSEMARY SYRUP

Summon a bit of lunar love in your life and your concoctions with this vivacious, endearing Rose, Jasmine, and Rosemary Syrup. Combining the bewitching moon magic of these two enchanting flowers with a tad of rosemary, this simple mixture can add a touch of aromatics and a beguiling light pink hue to your creations. Energetically, this syrup is great for lunar libations inviting love, psychic abilities, healing, and spirituality. If you don't have access to organic jasmine flowers, feel free use solely rose and rosemary.

Yields $^3/_4$ cup

$^1/_2$ cup water
$1^1/_2$ tablespoons dried rose petals
$^1/_2$ tablespoon dried jasmine
1 sprig fresh rosemary
$^1/_2$ cup granulated sugar

1. Boil water in a small pot over high heat. While waiting for water to boil, place rose petals, jasmine, and rosemary in a small, heatproof jar. Take a moment to enjoy their scent and tune in to their spiritual and healing energies.

2. Pour boiling water over flowers and allow to steep 5 minutes. Stir in sugar. Allow to cool 10 minutes, then strain, cover, and store in refrigerator until ready to use, up to 1 month.

SHRUBS

Shrubs, also referred to as "drinking vinegars," are essentially mixtures of vinegar, sugar, and flavoring ingredients like fruits and vegetables. On occasion, spices and herbs may be added. Beyond the preservation of healing remedies, shrubs have historically been used to aid and cleanse the digestive tract, similar to kombucha. Today, shrubs can be used to add an extra layer of magic and flavor to mixed drinks. The following recipe is used to create a number of moon-aligned cocktails in Part 2.

BALSAMIC MOON SHRUB

In alcohol and magical mixology, the energies of grapes are often utilized through wine. However, the nuanced flavors and lunar potency of grape have so much more to offer beyond that! Enjoy the luscious flavors of grape and other moon-associated ingredients like lemon and rosemary in this potent, rich recipe. Packed with lunar power for healing, purification, improving mood, and strengthening the mind, this enchanting Balsamic Moon Shrub is perfect to enjoy when preparing for lunar work, cleansing the mind for visualization, or for healing and releasing.

Yields 1 cup

$1/2$ cup red grapes
1 lemon peel
1 sprig fresh rosemary
$1/4$ cup amber honey
2 tablespoons water
$1/4$ cup balsamic vinegar

1. In a small bowl, muddle together grapes, lemon peel, rosemary, and honey. Once grapes have been mashed, add water and transfer to a small pot over medium heat. Bring to a boil, then let simmer and reduce 10 minutes.

2. Remove pot from stove and let mixture cool 10 minutes. Add vinegar and transfer to a Mason jar. Cover and refrigerate 3 weeks, then strain out solids before using. Shrub will last up to 6 months.

INFUSIONS

Infusing alcohol with herbs was once a prominent way for folk healers and doctors to preserve medicinal herbal essences that otherwise wouldn't last in a time with no refrigeration. In modern magic, infusions are still used to help preserve the energetic effects of different ingredients and are commonly added to rose waters as well as solar and lunar waters and mists. Yet in the craft cocktail world, infusing ingredients into alcohol has turned from a purely medicinal process into one that also happens to taste delicious. When you infuse something like tequila with cucumber, an ordinary drink turns into an even more refreshing and magically aligned concoction. In the following section, you will combine the best of both worlds to craft delicious and magical infusions that will add layers of lunar magic to any concoction. You can even try using these infusions in a lunar mist!

How to Infuse

Infusing is simple and also fun! Just add an ingredient or blend of ingredients to a jar with the alcohol of your choice, and wait. Every ingredient takes a different amount of time to infuse, so taste your infusion every few hours or every day until it has reached the desired flavor.

In the recipes that follow, you will find lunar-specific infusions to help draw down and strengthen various associations of the moon in your cocktails. For extra moon magic, let them infuse under the full moon just like you would moon water!

CUCUMBER TEQUILA

Add some lunar zest to your margarita with this Cucumber Tequila infusion. Combining the beauty and youth associations of agave and cucumber, this recipe makes a refreshing addition to your tequila-based drinks. Revel in the restorative, rejuvenating energies of both these powerful ingredients and call down the beautifying light of the moon in your cosmic potions.

Yields 1 cup

$2/3$ cup peeled and thinly sliced cucumber

1 cup blanco tequila

Place cucumber in a small jar and pour tequila over cucumber. Seal jar and shake, then allow to sit at room temperature 48 hours. Strain and discard solids, or keep as a booze-infused cocktail garnish. Store infused alcohol out of light at room temperature up to 3 months.

VANILLA VODKA

A delightful addition to everything from pumpkin martinis to White Russians, the enticing and calming flavors of vanilla-infused vodka can elevate numerous cocktails. Add to lunar libations for money or sexuality, or to inspire peace.

Yields 1 cup

1 (2") piece vanilla bean
1 cup vodka

Split vanilla bean and place in a jar. Pour in vodka and allow to sit 48 hours at room temperature. Strain out solids, discarding vanilla bean or keeping to reuse for a vanilla syrup if desired. Store in a dark place at room temperature up to 3 months.

BITTERS

From celery and chocolate flavors all the way to applewood smoked, there is a seemingly never-ending array of new and exciting bitters in the craft cocktail world. A highly condensed tincture of alcohol mixed with different ingredients such as herbs and sugar, bitters can add a powerful kick of flavor and completely transform the balance of a drink with just a few drops. The origins of bitters are similar to those of shrubs and infusions: They were created as a method of extracting and preserving herbal essences for medicinal purposes. While some bitters are easier to purchase, others can be made at home with a few simple steps and ingredients. The recipes that follow are used in a number of the drinks in Part 2. Look online or in your local liquor store for other bitters used in the lunar cocktail recipes.

LAVENDER BITTERS

Lavender has enchanted many with its calming and soothing scent. This herb makes a great bitters ingredient! You really can't go wrong when adding a touch of this floral, peaceful essence to any concoction. Use when wishing to add a sense of tranquility in your lunar potions, to help promote proper communication and harmony, and to enhance your innate intuitive abilities.

Yields $^2/_3$ cup

1 tablespoon dried lavender flowers
$^1/_3$ cup Everclear
1 ounce hot water
2 tablespoons granulated sugar

1. Place lavender in a small jar and pour Everclear over it. Cover jar and allow to sit at room temperature 3 weeks, shaking every day or so. After 3 weeks, strain out and reserve solids and set infused alcohol aside.

2. Place solids in a small bowl or jar, and pour hot water over. Allow to steep 5 minutes, then stir in sugar. Refrigerate overnight, then strain out solids and mix syrup into alcohol infusion. Pour into a dropper bottle. Bitters should last up to 1 year in a cool, dark place.

MOON DROP BITTERS

While jasmine is a potent herb for a variety of lunar workings—abundance, creativity, communication, peace, and intuition—the flavor can often be overwhelming. Combined with peach for love, ginger for success and power, and nutmeg for luck and money, the magic of the moon and jasmine can be celebrated in an endless (and tasty) array of potions. Using this fruity, floral, and spiced bitters recipe, you can add a kick of moon power to your potions for love, money, and wisdom, with the added bonus of luck and success.

Yields $1/2$ cup

2 dried peach slices, diced
1 teaspoon peeled and diced ginger
$1/8$ teaspoon dried jasmine flowers
$1/16$ teaspoon ground nutmeg
$1/3$ cup Everclear
2 tablespoons hot water
2 tablespoons granulated sugar

1. Place peach, ginger, jasmine, and nutmeg in a small jar and pour Everclear on top. Cover jar and allow to sit at room temperature in a dark place 3 weeks, shaking every day or so. After 3 weeks, strain out and reserve solids and set infused alcohol aside.

2. Place solids in a small bowl or jar, and pour hot water over. Allow to steep 5 minutes, then stir in sugar. Refrigerate overnight, then strain out solids and mix syrup into alcohol infusion. Pour into a dropper bottle. Bitters should last up to 1 year in a cool, dark place.

LUNAR LIQUEURS

From Kahlúa to Cointreau, the ever-growing array of liqueurs has established a central role in the world of mixology. And while these brand names may have a permanent place in the cocktail kingdom, it is actually relatively simple to craft some of your own at home. Essentially, liqueurs are a blend of sugar, alcohol, and flavoring ingredients. These make great alternatives to store-bought versions when you want to add even more moon magic to your drinks.

In the following section, you will find homemade liqueur recipes that will help draw down the moon in your own potent potions. Use these recipes as is, or as inspiration for your own unique creations. Some liqueurs are more difficult to create at home than others; check your local liquor store for liqueurs used in Part 2 that aren't included as recipes in this section. You can also find premade versions of these recipes in stores if preferred.

BLACKBERRY LIQUEUR

Call down the moon's power for healing, protection, and sensuality with this homemade Blackberry Liqueur. Using moon-associated blackberry to add lunar potency, this silky sweet, fruity liqueur is an easy go-to during blackberry season. Blackberry is also associated with the goddess Brigid, who is known especially for inspiring creativity and for her healing abilities.

Yields 1^1/$_2$ cups

2 cups fresh blackberries
1 cup vodka
^{1}/$_3$ cup granulated sugar
^{1}/$_3$ cup water
1 tablespoon dry red wine

1. Add blackberries to a jar and muddle. Pour in vodka, close jar, and set aside at room temperature in a dark place, shaking once a day for 5 days.

2. In small pot over medium heat, add sugar and water and stir. Bring to a boil 5 minutes, then remove from heat and let cool 10 minutes. Place in jar with vodka, add red wine, and let sit in a cool, dark place 24 hours. Strain out solids and store in a cool, dark place up to 1 month.

LUNAR LIMONCELLO

The beauty of combining the moon and mixology is that one ingredient in particular happens to be essential in a number of cocktails and is also associated with the moon: lemons! Call down the revitalizing, jovial, and purifying energy of the moon with this succulent, luscious, and invigorating limoncello recipe. It's the perfect beverage to enjoy with some sparkling white wine, soda water, or punch at a moon gathering.

Yields 1³/₄ cups

Peels of 3 medium lemons
1 cup vodka
³/₄ cup water
³/₄ cup granulated sugar
1 tablespoon dried or fresh rose petals

1. Place lemon peels in a large glass jar and cover with vodka. Allow to sit 10 days, shaking every day or so.

2. Add water, sugar, and rose petals to a small pot over medium heat. Bring to a boil, stir, then remove from heat and stir in lemon infusion. Let cool 10 minutes, transfer to a jar, and allow to sit 24 hours, then strain out solids. Store in a cool, dark place up to 1 month.

VIOLET LIQUEUR

Violet Liqueur, or crème de violette, is a favorite for its charming hue and enchanting floral fragrance and taste. Violet Liqueur is a great way to get the peace, hope, and psychic associations of this magical flower into many lunar libations. Add to potions for lunar dreaming, peace, and inspiring love, or simply to add a touch of magical appeal. While this homemade variation may not have the depth of purple color found in store-bought versions, you can always add $1/2$ tablespoon dried butterfly pea flower for a deeper hue.

Yields 1$^1/_4$ cups

1 cup dried purple violets
1 cup water
1 cup granulated sugar
1 lemon peel
1 teaspoon dried lavender flowers
1 (1") piece vanilla bean, split open
1 cup gin
1 teaspoon butterfly pea flower

1. Heat violets, water, sugar, lemon peel, lavender, and vanilla bean in a small pot over medium heat until boiling. Stir, then remove from heat.

2. Stir in gin and butterfly pea flower, allow to cool 10 minutes, then transfer to a jar. Infuse 24 hours in a cool, dark place before straining out solids. Store in a cool, dark place up to 1 month.

PART 2

LUNAR LIBATIONS

Now that you have learned the various tools and ingredients that come into play with magical moon mixology, you are ready to craft your own lunar libations! Here, you will find cosmic concoctions aligned to the moons of each season. Each recipe also offers an additional way to elevate the magic of the drink. Garnishes can be swapped or added for specific magical associations (see Appendix B: Edible Element Associations for guidance). And since seasons are opposite in the Southern and Northern Hemispheres, see the "Moon(s)" section in each recipe for all moons you can enjoy that drink under. No need to wait for winter to enjoy that enchanted eggnog!

CHAPTER 5

FALL
LUNAR
LIBATIONS

As summer transitions to fall, the hours of daylight decrease and night begins its long reign. Grains, herbs, and certain fruits, such as grapes for wine, are harvested, and cele-brations ensue. Cycles of life and death take center stage. Reflective of these seasonal themes, the fall moons high-light harvest, abundance, transitions, and endings. Lighting its way through all the signs, but emphasizing Aries, Libra, Scorpio, Taurus, Sagittarius, and Gemini with its new and full cycles, the fall moon represents transformation and passion through wisdom, action, and balance.

The recipes in this chapter harness these powers of the fall moons but can be enjoyed at any time of year. From a Lunar Purification Potion to purify with the waning moon, to a Pumpkin Spice Lunar Latte for abundance, there's a deli-cious lunar concoction for whatever you desire.

COSMIC EMBRACE

ENERGIES: comfort, the home, grounding, love

MOON(S): in Taurus, in Libra, in Pisces, waning moons

As the weather shifts, the Taurus moon invites us to bathe in creature comforts and refocus on the home and our sense of security and stability in order to take us through the winter months. With Taurus-ruled vanilla, this spiced brandy is the perfect concoction to sip during a cold night under the Taurus moon. Using soothing and grounding ingredients, this cocktail will help you call down the Taurus moon for love, warmth, and comfort through whatever transitions and weather the fall moons bring.

Serves 1

5 ounces water
1 tablespoon butter, softened
$1/2$ tablespoon vanilla extract
$1/2$ tablespoon dried rose petals
$1/2$ ounce Honey Syrup (see recipe in Chapter 4)
$1/8$ teaspoon salt
$1/8$ teaspoon ground cardamom
2 ounces brandy

Boil water in a small pot over high heat. Meanwhile, place remaining ingredients except brandy in a tempered mug. Muddle butter in spices and sweeteners, envisioning your own body relaxing with each muddle. Pour in hot water, then brandy.

More Moon Magic

A symbol of abundance and sustenance, the bull knows when to rest in the pastures and when to pursue something with determination. The moon in Taurus offers an opportunity to reflect on the balance of comfort and productivity. Do you take the time to rest and enjoy creature comforts? Is your home set up as a space of security? Meditate on the bull, breathing deeply between sips of your cocktail, and see what messages arise for you.

LUNAR PURIFICATION POTION

ENERGIES: purification, healing, mood

MOON(S): third quarter moon, waning moons

Draw down the potency of the moon to cleanse your energy with this crisp, refreshing rosemary and grapefruit spritzer. With the herbal base of gin, rosemary, and grapefruit for purification, elevated with soothing honey, floral rose, and bubbling sparkling wine, this concoction will revitalize your energy. Delight in this beverage to call down the light of the moon, to cleanse your energy during the waning moon, or to prepare for the coming new moon.

Serves 1

1 sprig fresh rosemary
3/4 ounce grapefruit juice
1 ounce gin
1/4 ounce Honey Syrup (see recipe in Chapter 4)
4 dashes rose water
2 ounces sparkling white wine

Place rosemary sprig, grapefruit juice, gin, Honey Syrup, and rose water into a cocktail shaker filled with ice. Shake the ingredients, also shaking away any negative energy. Strain into a coupe glass with 1 large ice cube/sphere, and top with sparkling wine.

More Moon Magic

To increase the energetic potency of this lunar libation, enjoy this beverage with a piece of selenite. As you sip the beverage, visualize the powerful essences of rosemary, grapefruit, and juniper cleansing your body as though with lunar light. Then use the purifying energy of selenite to help you release any negative energy by waving it through your aura or above your body.

MOON MATCHA

ENERGIES: balance, self-care, love

MOON(S): in Libra, in Taurus, waning moons

Imbibe the energies of the Libra moon for inner love and self-care with this rose and vanilla matcha. Ruled by Venus, the Libra moon is a time of loving, artistic, and romantic energies. At the same time, the scales by which this sign is represented reflect a moment of balance of emotional and subconscious energies. The moon in this sign can be a time to look inward at your own inner sense of balance. Enjoy when the moon is in Libra, or any time you wish to imbibe some lunar-inspired emotional balance, love, and healing. For a nonalcoholic version, omit the Vanilla Vodka.

Serves 1

1 cup oat milk
1 teaspoon matcha green tea powder
1 tablespoon pure maple syrup
2$\frac{1}{4}$ teaspoons dried rose petals, divided
$\frac{1}{8}$ teaspoon ground cardamom
$\frac{1}{8}$ teaspoon ground nutmeg
1 ounce Vanilla Vodka (see recipe in Chapter 4)

1. Pour oat milk into a small pot and warm over medium heat 5 minutes or until warm. Stir in matcha, maple syrup, 1$\frac{1}{8}$ teaspoons rose petals, cardamom, and nutmeg. Let simmer 3 more minutes.

2. Once mixed and hot, pour into a mug with Vanilla Vodka and garnish with remaining 1$\frac{1}{8}$ teaspoons rose petals.

—◇—●—————— More Moon Magic ——————●—◇—

Further the energy of this soothing Moon Matcha with some amethyst-aided introspection. Grab your lunar beverage and sit under the luminous rays of the Libra moon, holding a piece of amethyst in your other hand. Breathe in the magic of the night, sipping your latte and tuning in to your body. Envision the supportive energy of the moon and the amethyst surrounding you as you drink.

LUNAR LUCK TEA

ENERGIES: comfort, vibration raising, luck
MOON(S): in Sagittarius, waxing moons, full moon

Warm up under the winter moonlight with this spiced Lunar Luck Tea. Inspired by the moon in Sagittarius, yet to be enjoyed any time of year, this grounding hot toddy can also easily be made into an iced tea. With spices like nutmeg and clove to raise your vibration for purification, good luck, and optimism, it will have you feeling positive about yourself and your chances.

Serves 1

$1/8$ teaspoon ground nutmeg
$1/8$ teaspoon ground clove
1 sprig fresh rosemary
1 small slice peeled fresh ginger
$1^1/_2$ ounces Honey Syrup (see recipe in Chapter 4)
5 ounces hot water
$1/2$ ounce lemon juice
1 ounce whiskey

Place nutmeg, clove, rosemary, ginger, and Honey Syrup in a mug. Muddle together until ginger is broken down. Add hot water and let steep 5 minutes. Top with lemon and whiskey.

More Moon Magic

Switching the more traditional orange for lunar-associated lemon, this pomander ball is the perfect way to amplify the luck, optimism, and spirituality associations of your cocktail. To make a Lemon Pomander Ball, puncture a large lemon with 40 whole cloves, then set aside. In a bowl or on a plate, mix together 1 tablespoon ground nutmeg, 1 tablespoon ground ginger, 1 tablespoon dried or powdered rosemary, and 1 tablespoon ground cinnamon. Roll lemon pomander ball into the mixture. Slide a long piece of wire through ball. Store ball in a paper bag about 3 weeks. Decorate wire with ribbon and hang ball over a doorway to purify the energy that comes in and invite good luck.

MAPLE MOON

ENERGIES: happiness, harmony, healing

MOON(S): in Libra, in Cancer, in Taurus

Symbolized by the scales, Libra is a time for balance in relationships of all kinds. Inspire teamwork, cooperation, or the energy of fairness with this sweet, autumnal maple and rose concoction. With earthy maple, loving rose, and peaceful rosemary, this beverage will help ground your energy under the moon and provide soothing and cooperative vibes. Serve in nonalcoholic form to people you are working with to inspire cooperation, or drink as a cocktail to call down the Libra moon for justice and harmony in your personal magical efforts. For a nonalcoholic version, skip the rum and brandy.

Serves 1

1 fresh strawberry, hulled and sliced
2 sprigs fresh rosemary, divided
1/8 teaspoon ground nutmeg
4 dashes rose water
1 tablespoon pure maple syrup
3/4 ounce lemon juice
1 ounce dark rum
1/4 ounce apple brandy
1 1/2 ounces soda water

In a bucket glass, muddle strawberry, 1 rosemary sprig, nutmeg, rose water, and maple syrup together, visualizing any problems being stamped out and harmony instead taking over. Add ice to fill, then stir in lemon juice, rum, apple brandy, and soda water. Garnish with remaining rosemary sprig to help inspire peace with each sip.

───── ◇─■────── **More Moon Magic** ──────■─◇ ─────

Roses are known for love but are also useful for peace: Their thorned stems deflect negativity, while their scent and beautiful flowers attract beauty and calm. Place white roses (or whichever color is most accessible to you) on your lunar altar and enjoy their beauty while sipping your cocktail, or have them nearby while you serve this drink.

ARIES MOON MULE

ENERGIES: lust, love, success

MOON(S): in Aries, in Scorpio, waxing moons

Trailing the end of summer and greeting the entrance of fall, the Aries full moon invites a key time for passion, for tying up loose ends, and, when properly directed, for motivation and action. This spicy, invigorating tequila-ginger mule is designed to help you pull down the Aries full moon to finish incomplete ventures before winter. Skip the tequila for a nonalcoholic version.

Serves 1

1/8 teaspoon ground cinnamon
1 sprig fresh rosemary
2 fresh blackberries
1/2 ounce Lemon Balm Ginger Syrup (see recipe in Chapter 4)
3/4 ounce lemon juice
1 jigger (1 1/2 ounces) blanco tequila
2 ounces ginger beer
1 lime slice, for garnish

1. In the bottom of a copper mug, muddle cinnamon, rosemary sprig, and blackberries in Lemon Balm Ginger Syrup, visualizing yourself breaking through to achieve your goals with this lunar magic like a ram breaking through barriers.

2. Stir in lemon juice while visualizing yourself cleaning out any stagnant energy, then add tequila, stir, and fill mug with ice. Top with ginger beer and garnish with lime slice.

More Moon Magic

Whether you are looking for more vitality and confidence to usher in success under the Aries moon, or hoping to add more passion to your love life, carnelian can aid you! While enjoying this luscious beverage, hold a piece of carnelian, envisioning yourself filled with that Aries moon invigoration. When done drinking, spend a few moments breathing deeply and focusing on that vision, then keep the carnelian with you for as long as you wish to utilize its power.

PASSIONATE MOON MARTINI

ENERGIES: love, lust, peace

MOON(S): in Scorpio, in Libra, full moon

Call down the moon and the stars for some Scorpio moon–inspired intimacy.
Utilizing the peaceful and sensual energy of passion fruit, with bold spiced rum
as the base and invigorating ginger, this variation of the classic Pornstar Martini
will have you feeling sexy and confident. You can also top the drink with
1½ ounces sparkling white wine and add some Blackberry Liqueur
(see recipe in Chapter 4) if desired. Enjoy with a partner, or anytime
the moon is in Scorpio for extra sensuality. For a nonalcoholic version,
omit the rum and substitute juice for the liqueur.

Serves 1

1 small slice peeled fresh ginger
½ ounce Simple Syrup (see recipe in Chapter 4)
½ ounce passion fruit liqueur
½ ounce pomegranate juice
½ ounce lemon juice
1 jigger (1½ ounces) spiced rum
2 slices candied ginger, for garnish

Muddle ginger with Simple Syrup in the bottom
of a cocktail shaker. Add passion fruit liqueur,
pomegranate juice, lemon juice, and rum. Add ice
to fill, shake, and strain into a coupe glass. Garnish
with candied ginger.

More Moon Magic

*With its deep red hue, and sensual and empowering energy, garnet is the perfect
stone to enhance and accompany the passion of this drink. Hold a piece of garnet
as you enjoy this cocktail, visualizing it inspiring confidence
and boldness with each sip.*

CACAO CRESCENT

ENERGIES: vulnerability, forgiveness, mood, open heart

MOON(S): waning moons, in Taurus, in Leo

The waning crescent invites a time of surrender and release. Comfort and warm your soul at this time and let go with this lunar boozy hot chocolate. With a bit of spiritual cinnamon spice and sweetening sugar, this warming cocktail promotes release and relaxation. Drink under the waning crescent moon to comfort your system into surrender, help you turn within, or soften your disposition for forgiveness. You can also try this drink with almond or coconut milk, or forgo the alcohol.

Serves 1

6 ounces whole milk
2 tablespoons dark cacao nibs
1 slice peeled fresh ginger
4 dashes rose water
$1/8$ teaspoon ground cinnamon
$1/2$ tablespoon pure maple syrup
1 ounce Vanilla Vodka (see recipe in Chapter 4)
1 cinnamon stick, for garnish

Place milk and chocolate in a small pot over medium heat. Stir, seeing the chocolate melt and feeling yourself relax with it. Mix in ginger, rose water, cinnamon, and maple syrup, then remove from heat. Pour into a mug, add Vanilla Vodka, and garnish with cinnamon stick.

More Moon Magic

Much like the drink itself, lepidolite can help promote emotional balance, serenity, and calm. While sipping this concoction, hold a piece of lepidolite, tuning in to your heart with each breath. Feel yourself relax and open up with each sip.

STORMY DARK MOON

ENERGIES: grounding, power, protection, purification
MOON(S): dark moon, waning moons, in Capricorn

Cleanse away the energy of others and reset your energetic defenses with this Stormy Dark Moon—a twist on the Dark 'n' Stormy. The waning to dark moon can be a powerful time for purification and protection, to ground and cleanse away the energy of the last month in preparation for the new month. With a bold Balsamic Moon Shrub, hex-breaking lime, power-inducing ginger beer, and cleansing gin, this concoction is great for purging away toxic energy and grounding yourself back into your body. For a nonalcoholic variation, make without gin and bitters.

Serves 1

1/2 ounce Balsamic Moon Shrub (see recipe in Chapter 4)
2 dashes Angostura bitters
1/4 ounce lime juice
1 jigger (1 1/2 ounces) gin
1 1/2 ounces ginger beer
1 sprig fresh rosemary, for garnish

Add Balsamic Moon Shrub, bitters, lime juice, and gin to a bucket glass. Add ice to fill, then top with ginger beer. Garnish with rosemary sprig for clarity.

More Moon Magic

Black kyanite can help one release negativity and toxicity and become balanced and centered within their own body and energy. Hold black kyanite as you sip your cocktail to let go of unwanted attachments and ground yourself back to the protective earth. You may also wish to run the black kyanite through your aura anywhere you feel particularly vulnerable.

THE MOONLIT PSYCHIC

ENERGIES: psychism, spirituality, banishment, endings

MOON(S): in Scorpio

Due to its closeness to Samhain and its own intense energies, the fall Scorpio moon certainly inspires a psychic vibration. With the descent to winter and the visible changing of the seasons, this classic, green-hued, and herbaceous cocktail (crafted by the author Ernest Hemingway himself) is perfect for celebration and using the Scorpio moon for introspection, transformation, and reflections on death and change.

Serves 1

1 jigger (1¹/₂ ounces) absinthe
4¹/₂ ounces sparkling white wine
1 whole star anise, for garnish

Pour absinthe into a coupe or martini glass and top with sparkling wine. Garnish with star anise.

—◇—•———— More Moon Magic ————•—◇—

In addition to being symbolized by the scorpion, Scorpio is also associated with the phoenix, a marker of transformation through fire. What better way to represent change during the Scorpio moon than through fire? Write down whatever you wish to banish on a piece of paper. Carefully burn the paper in a fireproof dish, tuning in to Scorpio for transforming and ending the issue. As the paper burns, drink your libation to instill the sense of cleansing and endings.

TAURUS MOON
STABILITY SOUR

ENERGIES: abundance, grounding, longevity, love
MOON(S): in Taurus, in Libra, waxing moons

The Taurus moon amid the fall harvest season invites an opportunity for focusing on long-lasting goals in finances, as well as in love and stability. This tart, exciting cocktail, with abundant and luscious blackberries and nutmeg, grounding whiskey, longevity-associated apple, and revitalizing lemon, is the perfect concoction to enjoy the lusciousness and abundance of the Taurus moon. Sip while you work some money magic, focus on long-term goals, or ground your energy with the changing of the seasons.

Serves 1

2 slices quartered apple, divided
2 fresh blackberries
$1/8$ teaspoon ground nutmeg
$1/2$ ounce Rose, Jasmine, and Rosemary Syrup (see recipe in Chapter 4)
$3/4$ ounce lemon juice
$1/4$ ounce elderflower liqueur
$1-1^1/4$ ounces bourbon

Add 1 apple slice, blackberries, nutmeg, and Rose, Jasmine, and Rosemary Syrup to a cocktail shaker. Muddle together, then add lemon juice, elderflower liqueur, and bourbon. Add ice to fill and shake. Strain into a coupe glass. Garnish with remaining apple slice.

More Moon Magic

Emerald helps open the heart for prosperity, confidence, and love, making it a great match for the regal Taurus energy of this drink. Hold a piece of emerald as you make or sip this beverage, visualizing a green light growing in your heart, inviting in abundance, luxury, and romance.

OCTOBER MOON REVIVER

ENERGIES: purification, spirituality, psychic abilities, renewal

MOON(S): October moon, new moon, dark moon, waxing crescent, in Cancer, in Scorpio

The October moon is a time of honoring life cycles and endings. With its closeness to Samhain and the spiritual energies of the full moon, this moon is often used for psychism and to contact the dead. Enjoy this revitalizing classic cocktail to help you embody a new sense of self or to help enhance your spiritual communication.

Serves 1

$1/8$ ounce absinthe
$3/4$ ounce anejo tequila
3 dashes rose water
$3/4$ ounce dry vermouth
$3/4$ ounce orange liqueur
$3/4$ ounce grapefruit juice

1. Rinse a coupe glass with absinthe. Discard absinthe.

2. Add tequila, rose water, vermouth, orange liqueur, grapefruit juice, and ice to a cocktail shaker. Shake, envisioning the light of the moon waking up the dead. Strain into rinsed glass.

More Moon Magic

Marigold flowers are often used to worship the dead in South and Central America. They also work as a complement to the orange liqueur and floral elements in this cocktail to give gratitude to the earth and the cycles of life. After using the drink for purification and spiritual attunement, meditate with and leave a bundle of marigolds outside under a tree as an offering of thanks.

THE GOLDEN MOON

ENERGIES: renewal, prosperity, strength

MOON(S): December moon, in Sagittarius, in Capricorn, waxing moons

Straddling fall and winter, the December moon brings a focus to renewal and the strength to make it through the cold months. And there is no better way to warm up and soothe the soul than with a fortifying cocktail celebrating the season's harvest! With winter-activating allspice, supportive bourbon, healing honey, and revitalizing lemon, this Gold Rush/Whiskey Sour variation is designed to invoke vigor, rejuvenation, and prosperity with the December moon.

Serves 1

3 bay leaves, divided
1 ounce Honey Syrup (see recipe in Chapter 4)
$^3/_4$ ounce lemon juice
$^1/_4$ ounce allspice dram
1 jigger (1$^1/_2$ ounces) bourbon
1 egg white
2 dashes Angostura bitters

Add 2 bay leaves, Honey Syrup, lemon juice, allspice dram, bourbon, egg white, and bitters to a cocktail shaker. Shake without ice, then add ice and shake again. Strain into a coupe glass, and garnish with remaining bay leaf for strength and granting your wishes.

More Moon Magic

Bay leaves are often used to grant wishes. On the bay leaf garnish from this drink, or a fresh leaf, write your wish for the new year. Then, light a green candle atop the leaf before the new year and keep it lit through January 1, or until it burns out. Place the bay leaf somewhere relevant, like your wallet for prosperity, or burn it once the candle burns out. Enjoy this concoction again whenever you wish to reinvigorate the spell.

PUMPKIN SPICE LUNAR LATTE

ENERGIES: the home, abundance, protection, psychic abilities

MOON(S): November moon

Celebrating lunar pumpkin and nutmeg, this is just the concoction to help you embody the November moon and focus on home matters. This drink also has lots of financial associations to carry you through the winter months with abundance, as well as spiritually energizing ingredients like cinnamon and clove to use for grounded psychic endeavors.

Serves 2

1 cup almond or coconut milk
3 tablespoons pumpkin purée
2 tablespoons pure maple syrup
1 tablespoon vanilla extract
1/8 teaspoon ground cardamom
1/8 teaspoon ground cinnamon
1/4 teaspoon ground clove
1/4 teaspoon ground allspice
1/4 teaspoon ground nutmeg, divided
1 cup freshly brewed coffee
3 ounces Vanilla Vodka (see recipe in Chapter 4)
1/2 cup whole milk

1. Heat almond or coconut milk in a small pot over medium heat. As it heats, stir in pumpkin, maple syrup, vanilla extract, cardamom, cinnamon, clove, allspice, and 1/8 teaspoon nutmeg. As you stir, enjoy their spicy, grounding aroma. Pour in coffee.

2. Pour into two mugs, then add Vanilla Vodka, splitting evenly between two mugs. Whip whole milk into a foam in a small bowl, then dollop onto mugs. Sprinkle on remaining 1/8 teaspoon nutmeg.

More Moon Magic

A once-rare and much-sought-after spice, nutmeg is often used for representing abundance, health, and fidelity. This spice can be used for endurance during the winter months. If you have a whole nutmeg, or even ground nutmeg, pray over it and keep it in a pouch for abundance on your lunar altar.

THE TWINS' CREATIVITY POTION

ENERGIES: creativity, the mind, protection

MOON(S): in Gemini

Utilize the Gemini moon and get your mind going with this caffeinated cocktail. With coffee to energize, whiskey to ground and inspire rebirth, hazelnut for creativity, and anise for clearing and communication, this earthy beverage will help spark some lunar energy and fruitful ideas! Enjoy under the Gemini moon, or whenever you wish to use the energies of this sign.

Serves 1

6 ounces freshly brewed coffee, cooled
$1/_2$ ounce hazelnut liqueur
$1/_4$ ounce anise liqueur
$1/_2$ ounce Irish whiskey
$3/_4$ ounce almond milk
2 dashes walnut bitters
$1/_8$ teaspoon ground nutmeg, for garnish

In a highball glass, mix together coffee, liqueurs, and whiskey. Add ice to fill, and top with milk and bitters. Sprinkle nutmeg on top.

More Moon Magic

To heighten the nutty associations of this drink, work with a walnut. Walnut is often seen as representing the brain because it looks like one. Under the Gemini moon, intentionally power a walnut to enhance your intellect and memory. Hold it as you sip your drink, then keep it on your desk, place it in your pocket, or put it in a charm bag with mint, nutmeg, anise, and lavender for added potency.

GEMINI MOON MINT JULEP

ENERGIES: insight, ideas, the mind, clarity

MOON(S): in Gemini, in Virgo, in Sagittarius, in Scorpio, waning moons, full moon

Invoke ideas and grounding energy under the Gemini moon with this mint julep. Blending grounding and clarifying bourbon; mindful mint and rosemary; and jovial, lunar lemon, this mint julep variation balances your energy for clarity, creativity, and ideas. Channel this Gemini energy into projects that require new ideas and problem-solving.

Serves 1

8 fresh mint leaves
2 sprigs fresh rosemary, divided
2 dashes Angostura bitters
1/4 ounce Simple Syrup (see recipe in Chapter 4)
1 ounce bourbon
1/4 ounce lemon juice
1 ounce sparkling white wine
1 sprig fresh mint
1 lemon wedge, for garnish

Muddle mint leaves, 1 rosemary sprig, and bitters with Simple Syrup in the bottom of a copper mug. Stir in bourbon and lemon juice, then pack in crushed ice and top with wine. Garnish with remaining rosemary sprig, mint sprig, and lemon wedge.

More Moon Magic

The color orange is associated with the energy center of creativity and can also be a grounding force. Burn a candle of deep orange color dressed with a pinch of dried rosemary as you sip your cocktail and contemplate the moon. Burn it whenever writing about your lunar-inspired ideas.

LUNAR ALCHEMY

ENERGIES: transformation, peace, restoration, spirituality
MOON(S): dark moon, waning moons, in Cancer, in Scorpio, in Pisces

Embrace transformation and change under the dark moon with the Lunar Alchemy. Utilizing the cosmic and color-changing magic of butterfly pea flower, this beverage will change right before your eyes. With spirituality- and psychic-associated coconut, hope-inducing Violet Liqueur, and cleansing gin, this cocktail is packed with transformative associations, helping you to embody change in a peaceful, powerful, and fun way.

Serves 1

1/2 ounce Lunar Transformation Syrup (see recipe in Chapter 4)
1/4 ounce coconut rum
1/4 ounce Violet Liqueur (see recipe in Chapter 4)
1 jigger (11/2 ounces) gin
1/2 ounce lemon juice
1 small slice coconut, for garnish

Add all ingredients except lemon juice and coconut garnish to a cocktail shaker filled with ice. Shake, then strain into a coupe glass. When ready to enjoy the transformative color change, add lemon and stir. Garnish with coconut.

More Moon Magic

Similar to this drink and the transformative magic of the moon, bismuth is a powerful ally for transformation change, alchemy, and also spiritual journeying among the physical, spiritual, and astral realms. Use bismuth to enhance the magic of this cocktail by holding it as you sip your drink.

SALTY MOON POTION

ENERGIES: cleansing, protection, mood boosting

MOON(S): dark moon, new moon, full moon, waning moons

The moon can often activate one's intuition, and the spiritual energies of fall may only heighten this connection. Many people often also use the cycles of the moon to refresh and reset their energy. Using blueberry for psychic protection, sage and grapefruit for cleansing, and salt to ground, this simple concoction is designed to help lessen this often overwhelming energy. Enjoy this cocktail when you feel psychically sensitive to the moon, to help activate a sense of peace and security.

Serves 1

1 grapefruit wedge, for rim
1/8 teaspoon salt, for rim
7 fresh blueberries, divided
2 medium fresh sage leaves
1/4 ounce Simple Syrup (see recipe in Chapter 4)
1 jigger (1 1/2 ounces) Cucumber Tequila (see recipe in Chapter 4)
2 ounces grapefruit juice
1 ounce soda water
1 sprig fresh sage, for garnish

1. Wet rim of a bucket glass with grapefruit wedge, then twist in salt in a shallow bowl and set aside.

2. In the bottom of a cocktail shaker, muddle 4 blueberries and sage leaves in Simple Syrup. Add Cucumber Tequila and grapefruit juice, roll from one end of shaker to the other, then strain into rimmed glass over ice. Top with soda water. Garnish with 3 skewered blueberries and sage sprig for a protective lunar snack.

———◇━●━━━ More Moon Magic ━━━●━◇———

Black moonstone is powerful for workings surrounding new beginnings, inner journeying, grounding, and protection. As you sip this concoction, hold and draw upon the energy of black moonstone to help you transmute negative energy into wisdom and boost up your protection for new beginnings with the new moon.

CHAPTER 6

WINTER LUNAR LIBATIONS

The moon rules the longer nights of winter with her ethereal glow, lighting the way through these dark months. Cold weather and harsh winds, freezing rain, and eventually snow set the tone for hermit-like behavior. The winter moons, as one might expect, bring a focus to the home environment, but also to the idea of rebirth—a theme that can set the tone for the growth of the spring and summer moons.

From the new beginnings of Cold Moon Eggnog to a creativity-inspiring Lion's Moon Martini, the recipes in this chapter draw on comfort, fresh starts, and new ideas. Reset yourself in the cocoon of winter through the energies of new and full Cancer, Leo, Aquarius, Virgo, Capricorn, and Pisces moons. Enjoy these cocktails during their corresponding moons, or whenever you need to call on a particular lunar power.

MOON AND SAND

ENERGIES: determination, ambition, grounding

MOON(S): in Capricorn, dark moon, new moon

The winter moons illuminate matters of endurance and strength during the colder months of the year, and the Capricorn moon in particular can be used to heighten this energy to manifest determination, grounding, and ambition. Capricorn can certainly be a merciless sign when it comes to what it wants, and what better concoction to celebrate that spirit with than a twist on the bold Blood and Sand? Barley-centric scotch, earthy shrub, seasonal blood orange, and action-oriented red wine make this drink a forward, bold go-getter like Capricorn itself. Enjoy under the Capricorn moon.

Serves 1

1/8 teaspoon ground cinnamon
1 ounce scotch whisky
3/4 ounce Balsamic Moon Shrub (see recipe in Chapter 4)
3/4 ounce dry red wine
1/2 ounce blood orange juice
1 lemon peel, for garnish

Add cinnamon, scotch, Balsamic Moon Shrub, wine, and blood orange juice to a cocktail shaker. Add ice to fill and shake, then strain into a martini or coupe glass. Garnish with expressed lemon peel.

More Moon Magic

Bloodstone can help promote courage, action, and endurance in achieving one's goals, making it a great addition for enhancing the lunar magic of the Capricorn moon. Hold the stone as you drink this concoction, visualizing success and feeling it flow through your veins. After finishing the drink, keep the bloodstone on your person to remind you of your determination.

COLD MOON EGGNOG

ENERGIES: beginnings, healing, money, protection, strength

MOON(S): January moon

Celebrate the seasonal shift with this lunar eggnog. With the newness represented in eggs, the manifestative potential of spices like clove, and warming Vanilla Vodka, this is the perfect concoction to welcome the new year. Enjoy cold to express the cold moon, or warm to heat the soul through the winter months.

Serves 4

2 cups oat milk
2 bay leaves
2 cinnamon sticks
$1/2$ teaspoon ground nutmeg
$1/2$ teaspoon ground clove
$1/2$ cup granulated sugar
1 egg white
4 egg yolks
$1/4$ cup Vanilla Vodka (see recipe in Chapter 4)
$1/4$ cup brandy
$2/3$ cup heavy cream

1. In a small pot over medium heat, warm milk, bay leaves, cinnamon sticks, nutmeg, and clove. While it warms, whisk in sugar and egg white until thoroughly mixed.

2. Remove warmed milk from stove, and slowly whisk into egg yolks in a medium bowl. Pour mixture back into pot and heat again over medium–low heat 2 minutes.

3. Remove from heat, let cool 3 minutes, then stir in Vanilla Vodka, brandy, and cream. Pour into two mugs.

More Moon Magic

Eggs are a symbol of rebirth, and often used for purification, divination, and protection. Gather a large egg, a small bowl of salt, paper or a bay leaf, a pen, and a candle small enough to fit inside the eggshell. With eggnog in hand, ponder what you wish to give birth to this coming year. Visualizing this, split the egg and discard the contents. Write your wish on the bay leaf or paper and nestle it in the center of the salt bowl. Place one eggshell on top and stand the small candle inside the shell. Light the candle and keep it within sight as you sip your cocktail.

WINTER MOON
OLD-FASHIONED

ENERGIES: strength, healing, perseverance

MOON(S): in Capricorn, in Libra, full moon

The magic of this drink extends far beyond its beloved flavors. In the nest of winter, the Capricorn moon highlights the importance of planning and having a firm foundation upon which to build lunar abundance in the spring. With oak barrel–infused rye whiskey offering endurance and grounding, cinnamon prompting motivation and spiritual connection, and rose syrup to soothe, this concoction is aligned to draw down the Capricorn moon for perseverance and healing.

Serves 1

1/16 teaspoon ground cinnamon
1 sprig fresh rosemary
Zest from 1 lemon peel
3 dashes Angostura bitters
1/2 ounce Rose, Jasmine, and Rosemary Syrup (see recipe in Chapter 4)
1 jigger (11/2 ounces) rye whiskey
1/3 ounce elderflower liqueur
1 cinnamon stick
1 lemon slice, for garnish

Place cinnamon, rosemary, lemon zest, bitters, and Rose, Jasmine, and Rosemary Syrup in an old-fashioned glass. Muddle. Add 1 large ice cube or sphere, then pour in rye whiskey and elderflower liqueur. Stir clockwise with cinnamon stick, then discard. Garnish with lemon slice.

More Moon Magic

Oak is an enduring, determined, and strong ingredient. To enhance the lunar magic of this concoction, source some oak bark, and after drinking your old-fashioned, hold the bark. Connect to the energy of the bark, and envision your own energy being infused with its strength like a tree.

CELESTIAL LOVE ELIXIR

ENERGIES: love, divination, longevity, magic

MOON(S): in Cancer, in Libra

The Cancer moon tugs at the heart strings, and while at times this may mean love, healing, and vulnerability, it can also remind you of aspirations that make your heart sing. Combining cleansing lemon, soothing apple, grounding maple, and creative-based Grenadine, this cocktail is designed to accompany Cancer moon magic that helps open your heart to healing, and remind you of your true aspirations and goals—the ones that are your bliss!

Serves 1

2 dashes rose water
$1/2$ tablespoon pure maple syrup
$1/4$ ounce Grenadine (see recipe in Chapter 4)
$3/4$ ounce lemon juice
$1/4$ ounce dry red wine
1 jigger ($11/2$ ounces) apple brandy
1 maraschino cherry, for garnish

Add all ingredients except cherry to a cocktail shaker. Add ice to fill, shake, then strain into a coupe glass. Garnish with maraschino cherry for optimism and good luck.

More Moon Magic

Just like this drink, rhodochrosite is a powerful tool not just for helping one open their heart to healing and compassion, but also to reconnect with the creativity of their inner child and the passion that sets their heart aflame. Hold a piece of rhodochrosite while you sip this drink, feeling your heart open more with each taste. When finished, close your eyes and bring your focus to the stone in your hand. What in your life also makes you feel excited, and invites your sense of passion and fulfillment? How can you honor that more in your life?

MOONLIT LION

ENERGIES: indulgence, prosperity, love, money

MOON(S): in Leo

Enjoy the luscious lunar energies of Leo with this delicious, creamy, and sweet Orgasm cocktail variation. Blending chocolate liqueur, a hint of almond, and dark rum, this concoction is grand for lunar abundance, self-love, and some well-deserved indulgence under the Leo moon. Enjoy anytime you want to bring out your inner diva. Substitute the amaretto for hazelnut, and limoncello for orange liqueur, if desired.

Serves 1

$1/2$ ounce crème de cacao
$1/2$ ounce amaretto
$1/2$ ounce triple sec or Lunar Limoncello (see recipe in Chapter 4)
$1/2$ ounce vodka
$1/2$ ounce half-and-half
$1/4$ ounce dark rum
$1/8$ teaspoon ground nutmeg

Place all ingredients in a cocktail shaker, add ice, and shake. Strain into a coupe or martini glass.

More Moon Magic

The Leo moon provides the perfect time to craft and charge an indulgent sugar scrub to use in your bath rituals throughout the next 6 months until the next Leo new or full moon. Enjoy a Leo Moon Chocolate Scrub in the bath and soak up the self-love while sipping your lunar cocktail. To make it, combine 1 cup loosely packed light brown sugar, $1/2$ cup coconut oil, $1/3$ cup almond oil, 2 tablespoons unsweetened cocoa powder, 3 drops coconut extract or essential oil, and $1/8$ teaspoon ground nutmeg in a medium container and store at room temperature for up to 6 months. Use to gently exfoliate your skin while in the bath.

SOLAR ECLIPSE SOUR

ENERGIES: purification, protection, grounding, spirituality

MOON(S): solar eclipse, in Leo

Solar eclipses can often act as doorways to new beginnings, signifying powerful change in one's life. With elements drawing on the moon and the sun, and a red wine float covering an otherwise bright color just like the moon covering the sun, this 1870 Sour variation is symbolic of the solar eclipse both in visual representation and ingredient alignment. Mix egg white to symbolize rebirth, cinnamon for vibration raising, and blueberry for psychic protection, and you have a concoction to help ground and protect your energy during this celestial event.

Serves 1

4 fresh blueberries
$1/8$ teaspoon ground cinnamon
$3/4$ ounce Simple Syrup (see recipe in Chapter 4)
1 ounce lemon juice
$1/2$ ounce pulp-free orange juice
1 egg white
1 jigger ($1^1/2$ ounces) bourbon
$1/2$ ounce dry red wine
1 lemon slice, smoked, for garnish

Muddle blueberries, cinnamon, and Simple Syrup together in a cocktail shaker. Add lemon juice, orange juice, egg white, bourbon, and ice to fill. Shake. Strain into a highball glass filled with ice and float red wine on top. Garnish with smoked lemon slice.

More Moon Magic

Ametrine is a combination of citrine and amethyst, largely as a result of amethyst slowly turning yellow and becoming citrine under high heat. This process itself mirrors the theme of solar eclipses: transition. Hold this crystal as you sip your cocktail for added wisdom, positivity, and good luck.

CANCER MOON
JASMINE & ROSE

ENERGIES: self-love, purification, spirituality

MOON(S): in Taurus, in Cancer

Inspired by the loving, healing, and spiritual magic of the Cancer full moon, this concoction uses spiced rum as the base to help sweeten your disposition to yourself, nutmeg to heighten your energy, and lemon to cleanse and rejuvenate. Elevated by the floral magic of jasmine and rose for love, psychic ability, and spiritual connection, this is an enchanting and elevating potion for bringing love into every aspect of your being and reconnecting with your spiritual center.

Serves 1

$1/4$ slice plus 1 round slice red apple, divided

$1/2$ ounce Rose, Jasmine, and Rosemary Syrup (see recipe in Chapter 4)

$1/16$ teaspoon ground nutmeg

$1/2$ ounce lemon juice

1 jigger ($1^1/2$ ounces) spiced rum

1 lemon peel, for garnish

1 dried rose petal, for garnish

Break apart $1/4$ apple slice and drop into a cocktail shaker, then add Rose, Jasmine, and Rosemary Syrup and muddle. Add nutmeg, lemon juice, and spiced rum. Add ice to fill, then shake. Strain into a coupe glass. Garnish by bending the lemon peel into a little "boat" that will float on top of the round apple slice in the drink, and carefully place rose petal in boat.

———— ◇—•—— More Moon Magic ——•—◇ ————

The Cancer moon is the perfect time to indulge in a bath, and luckily the fresh herbs of this drink can help with that! Put a mixture of dried jasmine, rose, and rosemary in a bath with some Himalayan salt and steep your body in the loving aromas and energies as you simultaneously enjoy the drink.

LION'S MOON MARTINI

ENERGIES: creativity, energy, the mind

MOON(S): in Leo, in Sagittarius

Revitalize your creativity, heighten your talents, and boost your energy under the lion's moon with this hazelnut and coffee martini. With inspiring ingredients like hazelnut and clove, soothing Vanilla Vodka, and of course coffee for energy, this luscious dessert concoction will have your mind filled with ideas.
Enjoy under the Leo moon to hone your unique talents.

Serves 1

$1/8$ ounce anise liqueur
$1/8$ teaspoon ground clove
$3/4$ ounce freshly brewed coffee, cooled
$3/4$ ounce Vanilla Vodka (see recipe in Chapter 4)
$1/4$ ounce hazelnut liqueur
$1/2$ ounce coffee liqueur
1 star anise, for garnish

Add an ice cube to a coupe glass and rinse with anise liqueur. Add clove, coffee, Vanilla Vodka, hazelnut liqueur, and coffee liqueur to a cocktail shaker filled with ice. Shake. Discard anise rinse and ice cube from glass, then strain drink into rinsed glass. Garnish with star anise.

More Moon Magic

Amber is powerful stone associated with creativity, sensuality, and empowerment. This fiery crystal is perfect for the Leo moon to help inspire new ideas and also instill confidence to express those ideas out in the world. Hold a piece of amber in one hand while enjoying your lunar libation.

STARBOUND CHERRY COSMO

ENERGIES: perspective, innovation, optimism

MOON(S): in Aries, in Gemini, in Aquarius

See things in perspective with this Aquarian cosmo. Replacing traditional cranberry with optimistic cherry bitters, this concoction will have your mind refreshed and your horizons expanded in the same way this drink was reimagined. Sometimes, we have to see something in a new way, with a sense of optimism, in order to make progress, and no moon is better for this than that in the rebel sign of Aquarius. Try this cosmo twist under the Aquarius moon, or whenever you need the moon's light to help you envision new perspectives.

Serves 1

3 small fresh sage leaves
2 fresh mint leaves
3 dashes cherry bitters
1/4 ounce Simple Syrup (see recipe in Chapter 4)
1 jigger (1 1/2 ounces) vodka
1/2 ounce lime juice
1/4 ounce cranberry juice
1/2 ounce Lunar Limoncello (see recipe in Chapter 4)
1 sprig fresh sage, for garnish

Add sage leaves, mint leaves, cherry bitters, and Simple Syrup to a cocktail shaker. Muddle, then add vodka, lime juice, cranberry juice, and Lunar Limoncello. Add ice to fill, shake, and strain into a martini glass. Garnish with sage sprig.

More Moon Magic

To enhance the magic of this cocktail, use peppermint essential oil diffused in a carrier oil such as olive oil. Before enjoying your beverage, rub the oil on your temples in a clockwise motion, imagining new insight and ideas entering your mind, helping you to see past your own internalized limitations.

PISCES MOON CHAI LATTE

ENERGIES: creativity, healing, spirituality
MOON(S): in Pisces, in Libra, full moon

The moon in watery Pisces invites a plunge into spirituality, healing, peace, and creativity. In fact, the Piscean moon is perfect for expressing spirituality and healing through art! Combining healing spices and milk, this golden chai latte will help you draw down the moon for lunar healing, warmth, regeneration, and artistic inspiration.

Serves 2

3 green cardamom pods
5 whole cloves
1 teaspoon whole black peppercorns
1 cinnamon stick
3 small slices peeled fresh ginger
2 cups water
1/2 teaspoon ground turmeric
1/4 teaspoon ground nutmeg
1 tablespoon black tea leaves
1 1/2 cups coconut milk
1/4 cup pure maple syrup
2 ounces Vanilla Vodka (see recipe in Chapter 4)

1. Add cardamom, cloves, and peppercorns to a small pot over medium. Break cinnamon stick in half and add to pot. Heat until fragrant, about 3 minutes, then add ginger, water, turmeric, nutmeg, and tea leaves, and allow it to simmer 10 minutes. Remove from heat.

2. Warm up milk in a separate small pot over medium heat. Set aside.

3. Stir maple syrup into tea mixture. Pour into two mugs, add Vanilla Vodka, and top with milk.

More Moon Magic

A stone of wisdom, spirituality, and expression, turquoise is the perfect companion for this warming beverage. Hold a piece of turquoise while imbibing this drink, perhaps while painting or drawing, and tune in to its soothing tones.

WISE MOON AMARETTO SOUR

ENERGIES: longevity, prosperity, relationships, wisdom

MOON(S): in Aquarius, in Virgo, in Taurus, in Gemini, full moon

As the ruler of our subconscious emotions, the moon can often influence our feelings about relationships during its different cycles—and the moon in Aquarius is no exception. As Aquarius is often viewed as a sign of detachment, this moon may accentuate matters of individualism within social constructs and circles, and this means it can also bring light to relationship imbalances. With pear, lemon, and elderflower liqueur, this soothing concoction can help bring wisdom, longevity, and optimism to relationships. It also has lots of associations with prosperity and money, so be sure to drink when working money magic in order to encourage out-of-the-box thinking in true Aquarian fashion.

Serves 1

2 pear slices

4 medium fresh sage leaves, divided

1/4 teaspoon ground nutmeg, divided

1/2 ounce Simple Syrup (see recipe in Chapter 4)

1/2 ounce lemon juice

1 jigger (11/2 ounces) amaretto

1/2 ounce elderflower liqueur

1 egg white

In a cocktail shaker, muddle pear, 3 sage leaves, and 1/8 teaspoon nutmeg in Simple Syrup. Add lemon juice, amaretto, elderflower liqueur, and egg white. Shake without ice, then add ice to fill and shake a second time. Double strain into a martini glass and garnish with remaining 1/8 teaspoon nutmeg and sage leaf.

More Moon Magic

Almonds have a myriad of uses, from bringing wisdom and success to inspiring love and compassion in relationships. Take the magic of almonds beyond this concoction, by either gifting candied almonds to a group or meditating with almonds to connect to their wisdom.

FEBRUARY MOON GIMLET

ENERGIES: purification, renewal, excitement

MOON(S): February moon

With the February moon, themes of purification, renewal, and excitement take center stage. Imbibe these energies with this lunar gimlet. Blending cleansing lemon, positivity-inviting grapefruit, clarifying and renewing gin, calming lavender, and elevated Rose, Jasmine, and Rosemary Syrup, this is a soothing, purifying, floral concoction to enjoy under the February moon.

Serves 1

1/4 grapefruit slice
1 sprig fresh rosemary
2 dashes Lavender Bitters (see recipe in Chapter 4)
1/2 ounce Rose, Jasmine, and Rosemary Syrup (see recipe in Chapter 4)
3/4 ounce lemon juice
1/4 ounce elderflower liqueur
1 jigger (1 1/2 ounces) gin
1 lemon peel, for garnish

Place grapefruit and rosemary in a cocktail shaker. Add Lavender Bitters and Rose, Jasmine, and Rosemary Syrup and muddle. Add lemon juice, elderflower liqueur, gin, and ice to fill, shake, then strain into a coupe or martini glass. Garnish with lemon peel.

More Moon Magic

While the image and name of flower agate itself may certainly inspire an excitement for the coming spring, the energetic properties of this stone make it a great ally to work with during the February moon. Flower agate helps to negate stress and restlessness as well as one's own inner fears. Hold flower agate as you sip your cocktail to use its magic.

BLUE MOON LUCK POTION

ENERGIES: chance, inspiration, luck

MOON(S): blue moon, full moon, in Pisces

What better way to celebrate the blue moon than with a deliciously aligned potion? With its bright hue and calming ingredients, this cocktail will help you draw down moon magic and manifestation.

Serves 1

7 fresh blueberries, divided
2 dashes Lavender Bitters (see recipe in Chapter 4)
1/4 ounce Rose, Jasmine, and Rosemary Syrup (see recipe in Chapter 4)
1 sprig fresh rosemary
1/4 ounce ginger liqueur
1/2 ounce lemon juice
1/2 ounce Violet Liqueur (see recipe in Chapter 4)
1 jigger (1 1/2 ounces) gin

Place 4 blueberries in a cocktail shaker and muddle. Add remaining ingredients except 3 blueberries, add ice to fill, and shake, thinking about the magic of the moon shaking things up in your own life. Strain into a martini glass and garnish with remaining 3 blueberries.

More Moon Magic

Celebrate the blessings and element of chance of this moon with a little wildflower-seed magic. After sipping your cocktail, hold some noninvasive wildflower seeds in the palms of your hands as you bathe in the magical light of the blue moon. When you feel ready, release the seeds, knowing the lunar winds will take them to grow where they are needed.

CELESTIAL TRANSFORMATION POTION

ENERGIES: the mind, health and healing, cleansing/purification

MOON(S): in Virgo, new moon, waning moons

Always transforming, always changing, the moon offers recurring occasions to hit the reboot button—especially when in structured Virgo. The Virgo moon presents the perfect time to focus on setting up and instilling new habits. Mixing agave for rebirth and celery for health, this herbal cocktail will help you empower yourself and your lunar workings for a fresh start.

Serves 1

2 small slices celery stalk
4 fresh mint leaves
1/8 teaspoon dried dill
1/8 teaspoon ground black pepper
1/4 ounce agave syrup
1 ounce lime juice
1/2 ounce dry vermouth
1 ounce blanco tequila
1/2 ounce soda water
1 sprig fresh mint, for garnish
1 lime wheel, for garnish

Add celery, mint leaves, dill, pepper, and agave syrup to a cocktail shaker. Muddle ingredients together, focusing on the mental associations of celery, mint, and dill to help you overcome road blocks and on rebirthing agave for a fresh start. Add lime juice, vermouth, tequila, and ice to fill. Shake, then strain into a collins glass over ice and top with soda water. Garnish with mint sprig and lime wheel.

―――•――――――――――― More Moon Magic ――――――――――•―――

Oftentimes, to restructure habits, one has to work at the very core of their mind. Golden apatite can help you uncover internal limitations that prevent action and change, encourage you to move through internalized fears, and instill the confidence to make lasting changes. While reflecting on what habits or new health structures you wish to set in place, hold and meditate with this crystal.

NEW MOON HOT TODDY

ENERGIES: hope, wishes, power, peace

MOON(S): new moon, waning and waxing crescents

Blending soothing honey to renew your spirit, whiskey to ground and center, ginger and nutmeg for power, and rose and violet for luck and wishes, this cocktail has everything you need to work the moon for spiritual power. Enjoy to attune to the new moon for spirituality and manifestation, restore your energy during the dark moon, or inspire hope and power with the waxing crescent.

Serves 1

1/2 tablespoon dried rose petals
1 small slice peeled fresh ginger
1/8 teaspoon ground nutmeg
1 sprig fresh rosemary
3 dashes Moon Drop Bitters (see recipe in Chapter 4)
1/2 ounce Honey Syrup (see recipe in Chapter 4)
3/4 cup hot water
3/4 ounce lemon juice
1 ounce whiskey
1/4 ounce Violet Liqueur (see recipe in Chapter 4)
1 lemon wheel, for garnish

1. Place rose petals, ginger, nutmeg, rosemary, Moon Drop Bitters, and Honey Syrup in a tempered glass. Pour hot water over ingredients and allow to steep 5 minutes.

2. Add lemon juice, whiskey, and Violet Liqueur. Stir, then strain out solids if desired. Garnish with lemon wheel.

More Moon Magic

With the moon dark in the sky but the knowledge of forthcoming light present, this can be a powerful time for setting intentions. Sit by your moon altar with a notebook and your cocktail. As you sip, contemplate your intentions for this lunar cycle. Write them down, and when you feel ready, light a white candle, envisioning it blessing your work.

MARCH MOON MILK

ENERGIES: love, fertility, spirituality, growth

MOON(S): March moon, in Gemini, in Taurus

The full moon that greets spring, the March full moon, oftentimes called the seed moon, brings energies of love, fertility, and both spiritual and physical growth. Celebrate the peaceful transition of seasons and reawakening of life with this moon milk recipe. Using pear for longevity and money, nutmeg for abundance, and vanilla for peace, it will help you embody March moon magic.

Serves 1

2 dashes walnut bitters
1 ounce muddled pear
1 ounce whole or almond milk
$1/8$ teaspoon ground nutmeg
$1/4$ teaspoon vanilla extract
$1/2$ ounce Simple Syrup (see recipe in Chapter 4)
1 ounce brandy
1 lemon peel, for garnish

Place bitters, pear, milk, nutmeg, vanilla extract, Simple Syrup, and brandy in a cocktail shaker. Add ice to fill, shake, and strain into a coupe glass. Garnish with lemon peel.

More Moon Magic

With its milky opaqueness, soft pink hue, and nurturing energy, pink chalcedony is a perfect match for this loving and spiritual moon milk. Hold it while you sip to harness its unconditional lunar love, compassion, and sense of optimism.

DREAM-TIME MOON MILK

ENERGIES: dreams, peace, spirituality, psychic abilities

MOON(S): in Pisces

The Pisces moon in particular invites a time of celestial and Neptunian dreams. And there's nothing that can put you to sleep quite like a poppy seed milk! Associated with the moon, poppy is great for creativity, peace, and sleep. Drink during this moon to expand your inner consciousness, dream big, and connect to the collective unconsciousness of the world.

Serves 1

2 1/2 cups hot water, divided
1/2 cup poppy seeds
2 1/4 teaspoons dried lavender flowers
2 1/4 teaspoons dried jasmine flowers
2 tablespoons amber honey
1/8 teaspoon ground nutmeg
1/8 teaspoon ground clove
2 ounces amaretto
1 cinnamon stick, for garnish

1. Pour 1 cup hot water over poppy seeds. Let cool 10 minutes, then cover and refrigerate overnight.

2. Place lavender and jasmine in a medium, heatproof glass. Pour in remaining 1 1/2 cups hot water and let steep 10 minutes. Strain poppy seeds from water and discard water. Place poppy seeds in a blender. Strain lavender-jasmine tea into blender, then add honey, nutmeg, and clove. Blend 5 minutes. Strain through a cheesecloth into a glass or mug. Add amaretto, garnish with cinnamon stick, and enjoy immediately, or store in refrigerator up to 2 weeks.

More Moon Magic

Inspire even more lunar dreaming magic with a little herbal dream sachet bag. Mix together equal parts anise seeds, dried lavender, jasmine, chamomile, and poppy seeds. Place ingredients in a drawstring bag and store under your pillow.

CHAPTER 7

SPRING LUNAR LIBATIONS

From the dew on newly budding flowers to the sun's growing warmth, life is reawakening. The spring moons bring a time of love, renewal, peace, growth, and excitement—an expansion in all areas as the world emerges from the cocoon of winter. The moons in Sagittarius, Taurus, Libra, Aries, Gemini, and Scorpio take center stage, guaranteeing an exciting ride with love, sensuality, abundance, and new ideas and perspectives.

The lunar libations in this chapter are sure to invoke a rejuvenated sense of self. Enjoy a New Moon Beginnings Sake with sake and cherry for excitement and expansion. Sip a Cosmic Centering Spritzer with bitter grapefruit and soothing apple to manifest fidelity in both love and goals. Or mix up a Lunar May Milk Tea Punch with lavender, ginger, and butterfly pea flower to tune in to the spiritual energies of spring.

LUSH LUNA

ENERGIES: sensuality, love, luck, happiness

MOON(S): in Libra, in Leo

Long worshipped as a source of love and emotion, the moon in Venus-ruled Libra can especially invite feelings of affection and excitement. Celebrate the sensual, healing nature of this moon with a magically enhanced twist on the classic Sex on the Beach. With sensual peach, happiness-inducing raspberry and orange, and loving rose, this refreshing concoction will elevate your mood.

Serves 1

5 fresh raspberries, divided

1 fresh strawberry, hulled and sliced

4 dashes rose water

1/2 tablespoon pure maple syrup

1 jigger (1 1/2 ounces) vodka

1 1/2 ounces pulp-free orange juice

1 1/2 ounces cranberry juice

1/2 ounce peach schnapps

1/2 ounce lemon juice

In a bucket glass, muddle 4 raspberries and strawberry in rose water and maple syrup. Pour in vodka, orange juice, cranberry juice, and ice to fill. Top with peach schnapps and lemon juice, stir, and garnish with remaining raspberry.

More Moon Magic

Invite even more love and happiness into your life with a little candle magic. After enjoying a few sips of your cocktail, adorn the top of a pink candle with dried rose petals, envisioning love and happiness pouring into your life. Place your hands on either side of the candle, allowing your chest to overflow with happiness and excitement. When you feel the candle is charged, burn it on your moon altar, keeping it in sight as you sip the rest of your drink.

NEW MOON BEGINNINGS SAKE

ENERGIES: creativity, happiness, abundance
MOON(S): in Aries, in Aquarius

Utilizing Aries associations through rejuvenating lemon, refreshing mint, positive cherry, and action-oriented ginger, this floral cocktail is the perfect companion for drawing on the power of the spring Aries moon for revitalization and initiation. Swap the sake and sparkling wine for soda water to make a nonalcoholic version.

Serves 1

4 whole sweet cherries, pitted
5 fresh mint leaves
2 thin slices peeled fresh ginger
2 dashes rose water
1/2 ounce Lemon Balm Ginger Syrup (see recipe in Chapter 4)
1/2 ounce lemon juice
1 jigger (1 1/2 ounces) sake
1 ounce sparkling white wine
1 sprig fresh mint, for garnish

Place cherries, mint leaves, ginger, rose water, and Lemon Balm Ginger Syrup in a cocktail shaker. Muddle, visualizing yourself breaking away from the old winter energies and adding new, fresh energies. Add lemon juice, sake, and ice to fill. Shake, then strain into a collins glass. Top with sparkling wine. Add ice to fill, then garnish with mint sprig.

More Moon Magic

Aragonite is a great stone to use with this concoction to inspire vitality and power and exciting new beginnings. After sipping your concoction, sit down with the aragonite in your hand. Close your eyes and breathe deeply, tuning in to the pressure of the stone in your hand with each breath. Visualize yourself renewed and enthusiastic for all that spring has to offer.

ASTRAL MOTIVATOR

ENERGIES: revitalization, action, optimism

MOON(S): in Aries, in Leo, full moon, waxing gibbous moon

Greeting the entry to spring, the Aries moon sees the world alight with life, growth, and excitement. Use the Aries moon to add some passionate, vivacious energy to your seasonal start with this elevated cocktail. This beverage utilizes ingredients like cherry, rose water, and orange to inspire optimism and passion. Swap out the alcohol for $2^{1}/_{2}$ ounces soda water for a nonalcoholic version.

Serves 1

3 thin slices cucumber, divided
4 whole sweet cherries, pitted
1 small slice peeled fresh ginger
4 dashes rose water
$^{1}/_{4}$ ounce Simple Syrup (see recipe in Chapter 4)
$^{1}/_{2}$ ounce lemon juice
2 ounces pulp-free orange juice
1 jigger ($1^{1}/_{2}$ ounces) gin

Place 2 cucumber slices, cherries, ginger, and rose water in a collins glass. Muddle in Simple Syrup, then add lemon juice, orange juice, and ice to fill glass. Add gin, stir, and garnish with remaining cucumber slice.

More Moon Magic

Often used to inspire passion and action, there is no better color to utilize the magic of the Aries moon than red. Dress a red candle with some dried ginger and hold it between your hands. Spend a moment visualizing more passion entering your life. Light the candle and enjoy the sensual flavors of your drink while it burns in sight.

TAURUS MOON MONEY-MAKER

ENERGIES: money, love, luxury

MOON(S): in Taurus

Taurus is a well-known earth sign for finances and stability. Combining these energies with spring's verdant growth, the moon in Taurus is a key opportunity to manifest wealth and luscious love. Mixing money and love isn't always a good idea, but under the Taurus moon, this twist on the Dirty Banana pairs the two in a delicious and potent way. Enjoy your creature comfort under the Taurus moon and call in abundance with this concoction of loving spices like cardamom, abundant banana, and sweetening spiced rum.

Serves 1

1 large frozen banana, peeled
$1/16$ teaspoon ground cardamom
$1/16$ teaspoon ground nutmeg
$3/4$ cup ice cubes
1 ounce spiced rum
$1/2$ ounce coffee liqueur
1 ounce oat milk
1 whole sweet cherry, for garnish

Cut one small slice from banana and set aside. Add remaining banana to a blender. Sprinkle cardamom and nutmeg on top, visualizing the blessings of lunar love and money coming into your life. Add ice, spiced rum, coffee liqueur, and milk. Blend, then pour into a hurricane glass. Garnish with reserved banana slice and cherry.

More Moon Magic

Ground yourself further in the vibrations of luxury and fidelity in love with an anointed moon candle. Use ground cardamom and nutmeg to dress a brown candle. Spend a moment with the candle, visualizing it as the earth and the spices on the candle as the seeds of blessings yet to be sown. Put the energy of your desires into the candle, then watch it burn under the Taurus moon as you sip your cocktail.

PINK MOON POTION

ENERGIES: beginnings, growth, love

MOON(S): April moon, in Capricorn, in Taurus

Celebrate the spring pink moon with this floral concoction that is pink just like its namesake! Using roots like beet and ginger to celebrate the new growth of spring (while complementing the floral liqueur), this refreshing, earthy spritzer is great to enjoy under the pink moon for new beginnings in love and growth, as well as during magic workings surrounding revitalization and longevity.

Serves 1

$1/2$ thin slice plus 1 slice peeled beet, divided
1 slice quartered red apple
1 sprig fresh rosemary
1 small slice peeled fresh ginger
$1/2$ ounce Simple Syrup (see recipe in Chapter 4)
$1/4$ ounce elderflower liqueur
1 jigger ($1^1/2$ ounces) gin
1 ounce lemon juice
1 ounce sparkling white wine

Muddle $1/2$ beet slice, apple, rosemary, and ginger in Simple Syrup in a cocktail shaker. Add elderflower liqueur, gin, lemon juice, and ice to fill. Shake and strain over ice into a rocks glass. Top with sparkling wine and garnish with remaining beet slice.

More Moon Magic

Ruby, with its heart-opening yet strengthening powers, can further enhance the energy that the beet and ginger offer this concoction. As you sip, hold a ruby stone and tune in to its vibration. Perhaps hold it to your heart and visualize it opening your chest and infusing it with love, strength, and confidence.

LIBRA LOVE
UNDER THE FULL MOON

ENERGIES: love, healing, attraction, psychic abilities, luxury

MOON(S): in Libra

Attuned to the Libra moon, this peach, thyme, and rose concoction can promote artistic appreciation for many of life's facets, including expressing yourself luxuriously. So adorn yourself in a new set of clothes, spray yourself with some rose water, and enjoy your cocktail to fall in love with all the nooks and crannies of your life. Replace the apricot liqueur or apple brandy and sparkling white wine with 4 ounces soda water or sparkling apple cider for a nonalcoholic version.

Serves 1

2 sprigs fresh thyme, divided

3/4 ounce peach purée

1/2 ounce Rose, Jasmine, and Rosemary Syrup (see recipe in Chapter 4)

1/4 ounce rose water

1/4 ounce lemon juice

1/4 ounce apricot liqueur or apple brandy

3 ounces sparkling white wine

In a mixing glass, muddle 1 sprig thyme in peach purée, Rose, Jasmine, and Rosemary Syrup, and rose water. Add lemon juice and apricot liqueur or apple brandy, stir, then strain into a champagne flute. Gently pour sparkling wine on top, and garnish with remaining sprig thyme.

―――――― More Moon Magic ――――――

As a stone associated with unconditional love, kunzite can help curate a loving, positive perspective and energy. While reflecting on your Libra lunar intentions as you sip this cocktail, hold a kunzite crystal to your heart, visualizing self-acceptance and love coming into every aspect of your life. Work with this stone until the next moon.

LUNAR FOCUS

ENERGIES: clarity, money, strength, success
MOON(S): first quarter moon, in Virgo, in Leo

With Earl Grey's bergamot for success and clarity, ginger to motivate and cleanse, and lemon to rejuvenate and invoke optimism, this iced concoction is designed to help you hone in on your lunar goals and invoke a sense of optimism. Use the power of the first quarter moon for refinement, decision-making, focus, and determination for manifestation with this lunar beverage.

Serves 1

1 small slice peeled fresh ginger
1³/4 ounces Honey Syrup (see recipe in Chapter 4)
2 bay leaves, divided
1 ounce scotch whisky
3 ounces chilled Earl Grey tea
1¹/2 ounces lemon juice
1 lemon wedge, for garnish

1. Add ginger and Honey Syrup to glass. Hold 1 bay leaf between your palms, visualizing your success with you intentions. Add to a collins glass, and muddle ingredients together, as you imagine stamping out any obstacles.

2. Add scotch for strength and determination, then pour in Earl Grey tea for success and focus. Add ice to fill, and top with lemon juice as though blessed by the moon itself. Stir the drink, watching the colors mix, and garnish with remaining bay leaf and lemon wedge.

More Moon Magic

Just like this drink, aquamarine promotes courage as well as clarity and insight. With aquamarine in hand and a notebook nearby, breathe deeply into your body. Take a few sips of your drink, inviting yourself to center as you savor each sip and tune in to the aquamarine in your hand. Ponder what actions you can take to accomplish your goals, and let aquamarine and the drink inspire new approaches.

STAR SLINGER

ENERGIES: spiritual duality, socialization, recognition, uplifting energy

MOON(S): in Gemini, in Sagittarius, in Leo, full moon

With a balance of sweet and sour flavors, there's no better lunar libation to contemplate your own inner dualities with than the Star Slinger. Blending cleansing gin, jovial cherry and pineapple, and truthful anise, this is just the beverage to use for social engagements as you work on expressing yourself and spending time with friends. This cocktail will have you feeling powerful.

Serves 1

5 fresh mint leaves
2 dashes Lavender Bitters (see recipe in Chapter 4)
$1/_4$ ounce Lemon Balm Ginger Syrup (see recipe in Chapter 4)
1 jigger ($1^1/_2$ ounces) gin
$1/_4$ ounce anise liqueur
$1/_4$ ounce orange liqueur
1 ounce lemon juice
$1/_4$ ounce coconut rum
$1/_4$ ounce tart cherry juice
$1/_2$ ounce pineapple juice
1 ounce soda water
1 sprig fresh mint, for garnish
1 sprig fresh lavender, for garnish

Muddle mint leaves with Lavender Bitters in Lemon Balm Ginger Syrup in the bottom of a cocktail shaker. Add gin, anise liqueur, orange liqueur, lemon juice, rum, cherry juice, pineapple juice, and ice to fill. Shake, then strain into a hurricane or collins glass over ice. Top with soda water and garnish with mint and lavender sprigs.

More Moon Magic

Call down the Gemini moon further with a citrus spritzer. Mix water, orange juice, lemon juice, and rose petals in a glass jar. Place outside at dawn, if possible, in the sunlight. Remove from light at midday, mix with vodka, then pour into a spray bottle. Use this spray before having guests over, or before going out for social occasions.

SCORPIO MOON ENCHANTMENT

ENERGIES: money, sensuality

MOON(S): in Scorpio

A time of intense, raw energy, the Scorpio moon is a good opportunity for going after goals and managing financial partnerships. Celebrate and embody this energy with a lunar twist on the Black Widow cocktail. Much like Scorpio, agave-based tequila can be an element of confidence and lust. Paired with blackberry, basil, and allspice, this juicy, sensual concoction is packed with associations of abundance, money, and lust.

Serves 1

4 whole, fresh blackberries, divided
3 large fresh basil leaves, divided
$1/8$ teaspoon allspice dram
$1/2$ ounce agave syrup
$3/4$ ounce lemon juice
1 jigger ($1^1/2$ ounces) blanco tequila

In a cocktail shaker, muddle 3 blackberries, 2 basil leaves, and allspice dram in agave syrup. Add lemon juice, tequila, and ice to fill. Shake, then strain into a martini glass. Garnish with remaining blackberry and basil leaf.

More Moon Magic

Further the raw lunar power of this cocktail with a purple allspice candle. Purple is often a color of magic, power, opulence, and transformation, making it a great match for this drink (not to mention the matching hues). Sprinkle a purple candle with ground allspice and charge it with the power of the Scorpio moon. Enjoy your Scorpio Moon Enchantment while watching this candle burn.

COSMIC CENTERING SPRITZER

ENERGIES: positivity, healing, love, protection, fidelity

MOON(S): in Taurus

Highlighting the bitter Italian aperitivo with elements of rhubarb, orange, and various herbs, the classic Aperol Spritz is a refreshing, crisp concoction. Add the complementary magic of grapefruit, elderflower, and apple, and you have a grounding cocktail to enjoy under the Taurus moon. Sip to attune to the Taurus moon for deepening the sense of connection within your relationships or just to feel grounded and centered in your own body. For a nonalcoholic version, replace the Aperol with a slice of rhubarb.

Serves 1

1 slice quartered red apple, peeled
1 grapefruit peel
$^1/_2$ ounce elderflower liqueur
$^1/_2$ ounce lemon juice
1 jigger (1$^1/_2$ ounces) Aperol
2 ounces sparkling white wine

Muddle apple slice with grapefruit peel in the bottom of a cocktail shaker. Add ice to fill, followed by elderflower liqueur, lemon juice, and Aperol, and shake. Strain into a white wine glass and top with sparkling white wine. Add 1 large ice cube or sphere.

More Moon Magic

Spring is a time of seeds, planted for future growth and abundance. Apple and lemon seeds in particular are often used in love and fertility magic. Collect the seeds from the apple and lemon used in this drink, allow them to dry, then powder them with nutmeg for fidelity, endurance, and abundance. You can plant these seeds outside as a lunar ritual, or keep them in a pouch for other magic workings.

THE ARCHER'S MOON
BAHAMA MAMA

ENERGIES: adventure, spontaneity, energy, motivation, thoughtfulness

MOON(S): in Sagittarius, in Leo, full moon

The spring Sagittarius moon brings the perfect opportunity for adventure, spontaneity, and travel! Plan your spring and summer trips while sipping this rejuvenating, activating Bahama Mama variation. With coffee liqueur to energize and orange and pineapple to uplift, this tropical cocktail is sure to get you dreaming of distant lands and considering spring and summer goals.

Serves 1

1 ounce dark rum
$^{1}/_{2}$ ounce coconut rum
$^{1}/_{4}$ ounce coffee liqueur
1 ounce pulp-free orange juice
1 ounce pineapple juice
$^{1}/_{4}$ ounce Grenadine (see recipe in Chapter 4)
$1^{1}/_{4}$ cups crushed ice
1 sprig fresh mint, for garnish
1 pineapple wedge, for garnish

Combine all ingredients except ice and garnishes in a shaker. Shake, then pour over crushed ice in a hurricane glass. Garnish with mint sprig and pineapple wedge.

More Moon Magic

Associated with the Sagittarius moon, labradorite is great to work with for intuitive development and spiritual quests. But beyond its psychic nature, it is often used for protection as well as seeking information. Keep it nearby as you sip your cocktail and plan your travels, and be sure to bring it with you when you go!

STRAWBERRY MOON SOOTHER

ENERGIES: abundance, positivity, creativity, love, relationships

MOON(S): June moon, in Leo

As the seasons shift toward abundance and a bright summer, why not celebrate with a refreshing, tropical strawberry cocktail? With the addition of honey as a nod to the buzzing bees and honey harvests, and seasonal strawberries, this drink is perfect to inspire that summer moon transformation and reflect on relationships. Skip the alcohol for an equally delicious nonalcoholic version!

Serves 1

1 fresh strawberry, hulled
1 thin slice peeled fresh ginger
1/2 ounce Honey Syrup (see recipe in Chapter 4)
4 dashes rose water
1 ounce coconut cream
1 jigger (11/2 ounces) dark rum
3 ounces pineapple juice
1/2 ounce pulp-free orange juice
1 pineapple leaf, for garnish
1 strawberry slice, for garnish

In a cocktail shaker, muddle strawberry and ginger in Honey Syrup. Add rose water, coconut, rum, pineapple juice, orange juice, and ice to fill. Shake, then strain into a hurricane glass packed with crushed ice. Garnish with pineapple leaf and strawberry slice.

More Moon Magic

Enhance the soothing energy of this concoction and celebrate the coming of summer with sweet orange essential oil. Orange is known for boosting happiness, and is also used for wellness, blessings, and spirituality. Place some orange essential oil into a diffuser and enjoy the aroma of optimism while sipping this concoction.

LUNAR MAY MILK TEA PUNCH

ENERGIES: psychic abilities, enchantment, abundance

MOON(S): May moon, in Pisces

During the May full moon, flowers are abundant all around, and life has resurfaced anew. This moon invokes a sense of enchantment, divinatory abilities, and sensuality and is also a time to celebrate abundance. With floral ingredients like lavender and the color-changing butterfly pea flower, complemented by soothing cream and Vanilla Vodka, this cocktail will help you call down the May moon for some lunar enchantment, abundance, and excitement of your own.

Serves 1

4 ounces water
1 teaspoon dried lavender flowers
2 small slices peeled fresh ginger, broken up
1 sprig fresh rosemary
2 dashes rose water
1 ounce Lunar Transformation Syrup (see recipe in Chapter 4)
3/4 ounce Vanilla Vodka (see recipe in Chapter 4)
1/2 ounce half-and-half
1 small ginger coin, for garnish

1. Boil water in a small pot over high heat. Place lavender, ginger slices, rosemary, rose water, and Lunar Transformation Syrup in the bottom of a tempered glass, then add boiling water and allow to steep 5 minutes.

2. Add Vanilla Vodka, followed by a handful of ice, then top with half-and-half. Garnish with ginger coin.

More Moon Magic

With its deep blue hue and psychic energy, lapis lazuli is a great companion for this cocktail. To enhance your intuition and sense of enchantment with this stone, hold while sipping the drink, perhaps while conducting a divinatory spring reading or prior to meditation.

MOON MIMOSA

ENERGIES: cleansing, optimism, celebration

MOON(S): waxing gibbous moon

The waxing gibbous is a time when the moon is almost full. You have refined your goals and pushed through some struggles during the first quarter moon. With uplifting lemon to promote fidelity to your goals, grapefruit to cleanse and affirm positivity, and sparkling white wine to elevate your intentions, this Moon Mimosa is perfect for celebrating future achievements as well as invoking continuance of your aspirations. Replace triple sec and sparkling wine with $1/2$ ounce pulp-free orange juice and 2 ounces soda water for a nonalcoholic version.

Serves 1

$1/2$ ounce lemon juice
1 ounce grapefruit juice
$1/2$ ounce triple sec
2 ounces sparkling white wine
1 lemon peel, for garnish

Pour lemon juice, grapefruit juice, and triple sec into a champagne flute and top with sparkling wine. Garnish with lemon peel.

More Moon Magic

Take whatever incense you like, perhaps jasmine or rose for the moon, and go to where you can see the moon. Contemplate its growth and beauty, knowing it will soon come to fullness, the same as your own aspirations. Feel the excitement of your goals coming to pass. Once you feel yourself radiating with this positivity and abundance, look at the moon and light your incense while thinking of your goals and dreams. See the incense rising into the air, bringing your prayers and intentions to the moon to hear your words. Enjoy your drink in this abundant state.

LUNAR STATE OF MIND

ENERGIES: communication, the mind, purification

MOON(S): in Gemini, in Virgo

The moon in Gemini is the perfect occasion to work on how you express yourself and project your thoughts into the world. And this minty blue beverage is a delicious way to open up your throat and clear your mind in order to do just that. Serve at your next gathering to entice open communication or to practice speaking up for yourself, or sip alone under the Gemini moon to clear and purify your mind.

Serves 1

5 fresh mint leaves, divided

2 dashes Lavender Bitters (see recipe in Chapter 4)

$1/2$ ounce Lemon Balm Ginger Syrup (see recipe in Chapter 4)

$1^1/2$ ounces lemon juice

1 ounce white rum

$1/4$ ounce blue curaçao

$1/4$ ounce coconut rum

1 lime slice, for garnish

Place 4 mint leaves, Lavender Bitters, Lemon Balm Ginger Syrup, lemon juice, white rum, blue curaçao, and coconut rum in a cocktail shaker. Add ice to fill and shake. Strain into a collins or red wine glass filled with crushed ice. Garnish with lime slice and remaining mint leaf.

———————— More Moon Magic ————————

Connecting the heart and throat chakras, amazonite promotes clear communication of one's feelings. This would be a great energetic companion for your cocktail when you're looking to set boundaries, particularly if you have been feeling like your voice and emotions tend to be run "over" by others.

SAGITTARIUS MOON FIZZ

ENERGIES: optimism, peace, excitement

MOON(S): in Sagittarius

Cleanse away stagnancy and invite in peace, optimism, and excitement with this Sagittarius Moon Fizz. The sage leaves cleanse, while cherry and cucumber renew and invigorate. With a hint of ginger for energy, this restorative concoction is perfect to invoke a fresh perspective with the spring moons. And, in traditional Sagittarius flair, it has a rising foam to awe.

Serves 1

2 whole sweet cherries, pitted
3 large fresh sage leaves
2 round slices cucumber
1/2 ounce Lemon Balm Ginger Syrup (see recipe in Chapter 4)
1 ounce lemon juice
2 ounces sake
1/2 ounce ginger liqueur
1 egg white
1 ounce soda water

In the bottom of a cocktail shaker, muddle cherries, sage, and cucumber in Lemon Balm Ginger Syrup. Add lemon juice, sake, ginger liqueur, and egg white. Shake once without ice, then fill with ice and shake a second time. Strain into a coupe glass and top with soda water so that the foam of the egg white rises above the glass, in pursuit of new horizons just like the Sagittarius moon.

More Moon Magic

Of the moonstone varieties, peach moonstone is known for being more soothing and optimistic. And in traditional Sagittarius moon fashion, it also invokes some lunar wisdom and insight. Enhance the peaceful and cheerful energy of this cocktail by holding peach moonstone as you drink it under the Sagittarius moon, inviting a fresh perspective with each sip.

MOON MEZCALITA

ENERGIES: health, motivation, vitality, protection
MOON(S): new moon, full moon, in Cancer, in Aries

Whether utilizing the last of the spring moons for rejuvenation, starting new healthy habits, or ushering in motivation, this ginger and melon Moon Mezcalita has your back. With the cleaning trio of salt, melon, and ginger, plus the power and energetic zest of agave, this cooling concoction is a great support for renewal, energy, and power.

Serves 1

2 lemon wedges, divided
1/8 teaspoon salt, for rim
2 small slices cantaloupe or honeydew melon
1/8 teaspoon ground nutmeg
1/4 ounce agave syrup
1 ounce lemon juice
1/2 ounce ginger liqueur
1 jigger (1 1/2 ounces) mezcal

1. Wet rim of a bucket glass with 1 lemon wedge, then dip into salt in a shallow bowl to create a half rim. Set aside.

2. In a cocktail shaker, muddle melon and nutmeg in agave. Add lemon juice, ginger liqueur, mezcal, and ice to fill. Roll from one end of shaker to the other, then dump with ice into rimmed glass. Garnish with remaining lemon wedge.

More Moon Magic

When looking to manifest an intention into the world, it is best to have a constant source of power by your side! To make a success sachet for lunar vitality, abundance, and health to carry with you as you pursue you goals, add the following to a small drawstring bag: ground ginger, nutmeg (whole or ground), lemon balm, and a dried orange peel. Take any intentions you wrote for the new moon and place them in the bag. Let the bag charge under the moon, then keep it on or nearby your person for the lunar cycle.

CHAPTER 8

SUMMER LUNAR LIBATIONS

As the sun sets over plentiful fields and verdant green hills and bees hum back to their hives, the summer moons usher in themes of harvest and celebration as well as a focus on relationships. All of life is brimming with energy and growth. Individualistic Aquarius, flamboyant Leo, steady Capricorn, nurturing Cancer, structured Virgo, and fluid Pisces impact the moons of these warmer months.

From Lunar Love Spell Sangria to the Moon over the Sea Breeze, the cocktails in this chapter encourage deepening relationship dynamics, having fun, and celebrating coming success. Invoke healing and empowerment with the Summer Moon Margarita, or enhance your magic workings around socialization with the vibrant Social Selenophile. While these recipes are made with summer moons in mind, they can be enjoyed any time of year.

LUNAR LOVE SPELL SANGRIA

ENERGIES: happiness, love, lust

MOON(S): in Cancer, in Libra, in Scorpio, in Taurus, full moon, waxing gibbous moon

When in its home of Cancer, the moon can be an opportunity to enhance one's love life and deepen relationships. With sensual lunar ingredients like blackberry, peach, nutmeg, and orange to inspire love and fidelity; and ginger, hibiscus, and rum for some heat, it will be hard not to fall in love—with this drink.

Serves 6

1 cup frozen peaches
1 cup frozen strawberries
1/8 teaspoon ground nutmeg
1 (750 ml) bottle red wine
4 ounces Blackberry Liqueur (see recipe in Chapter 4)
2 ounces dark rum
2 ounces orange juice
2 ounces hibiscus tea
4 ounces Rose, Jasmine, and Rosemary Syrup (see recipe in Chapter 4)
6 ounces ginger ale

Place peaches, strawberries, and nutmeg in a bowl. Pour wine, Blackberry Liqueur, rum, orange juice, and hibiscus tea on top. Add Rose, Jasmine, and Rosemary Syrup and stir ingredients together clockwise, visualizing love coming into your life. Cover and let sit in the refrigerator overnight, then serve in six red wine glasses topped with ginger ale.

More Moon Magic

Make an attracting sugar jar with the following ingredients: sugar, dried hibiscus, dried lavender, ground nutmeg, ground ginger, and dried rose petals. Under the waxing or full moon, place enough sugar in a small jar to almost fill it, then add a pinch of each herb. Mix the herbs and sugar together, visualizing love and lust coming into your life. Draw a heart in the sugar with your finger. On a piece of paper, write what it is you are drawing toward you. Fold the paper toward you and nestle it in the sugar. Cover the jar and burn a pink or red candle on it.

MOON BLESSING

ENERGIES: blessings, happiness, purification, spirituality

MOON(S): July moon, in Cancer, in Leo

Utilizing coconut for purification and spiritual connection, spiced rum to help sweeten the soul, and pineapple and lemon for creativity and optimism, this Moon Blessing is sure to rejuvenate your spirit. Enjoy under the summer moons for blessing, spirituality, and optimism, or any occasion in which you wish to strengthen your spiritual connection to the moon.

Serves 1

1¹/₂ ounces spiced rum
¹/₂ ounce apple brandy
¹/₈ teaspoon ground nutmeg
1¹/₂ ounces coconut cream
3 dashes Lavender Bitters (see recipe in Chapter 4)
¹/₄ teaspoon dried rosemary
1 ounce pineapple juice
¹/₂ ounce lemon juice
³/₄ ounce Rose, Jasmine, and Rosemary Syrup (see recipe in Chapter 4)
1¹/₄ cups ice cubes
1 pineapple wedge, for garnish
1 pineapple leaf, for garnish
1 fresh rose petal, for garnish

Pour all ingredients except garnishes into a blender. Blend until smooth. Pour into a hurricane glass and garnish with pineapple wedge, pineapple leaf, and rose petal.

More Moon Magic

Revealing flashes of color as it is turned, opal is a great stone to use when working with the moon. It inspires one to dream big, enhances psychic abilities, and helps one release fear. Hold or meditate on opal as you sip your drink.

SUMMER MOON MARGARITA

ENERGIES: healing, beauty, empowerment

MOON(S): in Cancer, in Aries, in Libra, full moon

With this soothing, tantalizing margarita, it's easy to imbibe the emotionally nurturing and beautifying associations of the Cancer moon. Combining seasonal lunar watermelon for healing, Cucumber Tequila for rejuvenation and beauty, and refreshing mint, this Summer Moon Margarita will inspire healing and empowerment. It is also a tasty companion for lunar beauty magic workings.

Serves 1

2 (1") cubes watermelon
7 fresh mint leaves
1/4 ounce agave syrup
4 dashes rose water
3/4 ounce lemon juice
1 jigger (1 1/2 ounces) Cucumber Tequila (see recipe in Chapter 4)
1/4 ounce Blackberry Liqueur (see recipe in Chapter 4)
1/2 ounce elderflower liqueur
1 small slice watermelon, for garnish

In a highball glass, muddle watermelon, mint leaves, agave syrup, and rose water. Pour in lemon juice and Cucumber Tequila, then add ice to fill, followed by Blackberry Liqueur and elderflower liqueur. Stir, then garnish with watermelon slice.

More Moon Magic

As you sip this concoction under the Cancer moon, hold a rose quartz stone in your left hand, noticing how its color matches the hue of the drink. Spend a moment observing the stone, then close your eyes, bringing your awareness to the stone to see what you feel from it. Breathe in deeply, and notice your emotions. Bring to mind what you like about yourself, perhaps writing it down. If any wounds arise, visualize pink light from the rose quartz filling your chest with love for your unique self.

MOON OVER THE SEA BREEZE

ENERGIES: cleansing, protection, discipline, focus, wisdom

MOON(S): in Capricorn

Named for its refreshing cranberry and grapefruit flavors, this twist on the Sea Breeze cocktail can help revitalize and refresh the mind for focus and wisdom. Use it to call down the Capricorn moon so you can cleanse away the mental chatter, curate energetic protection, and enhance your focus to get projects done.

Serves 1

1 ounce vodka
1/4 ounce ginger liqueur
1 ounce cranberry juice
3/4 ounce grapefruit juice
1 grapefruit slice, for garnish

Add vodka, ginger liqueur, cranberry juice, and grapefruit juice to a bucket glass. Add ice to fill. Garnish with grapefruit slice.

More Moon Magic

Symbolized by the sea goat, the Capricorn sign embodies the determination of a goat with the flexibility and wisdom of a sea creature. After relaxing with a few sips of this concoction, sit in a quiet place and hold a piece of fluorite in your hand. With each breath, tune in to and relax your body, and bring your awareness to feel the pulsation of the crystal. Call to mind the image of the sea goat. Watch how it can navigate the tides and climb the tallest mountains. See what wisdom it has to offer you on your situation.

LUNAR LUXURY

ENERGIES: abundance, money, power
MOON(S): in Capricorn, waxing moons, full moon

Invite in lunar abundance and power with this spiced, shrub-based rum and elderflower concoction. Aligned to the Capricorn moon for prosperity and abundance, it will help you draw in the luxury.

Serves 1

$1/8$ teaspoon ground cinnamon
$1/2$ ounce Balsamic Moon Shrub (see recipe in Chapter 4)
$1/4$ ounce elderflower liqueur
1 ounce spiced dark rum
3 red grapes, for garnish

Pour cinnamon, Balsamic Moon Shrub, elderflower liqueur, and rum into a shaker with ice. Shake and strain into a martini glass. Add ice to fill. Stir and garnish with skewered grapes for a luxurious snack.

More Moon Magic

Cinnamon is often used for manifestation and inviting in money. Take a green candle and anoint it with oil, then coat it with ground cinnamon, visualizing money and abundance coming your way as you do. Hold the candle and imagine a goat bringing gifts and abundance to you. Light the candle and watch it burn as you sip your cocktail.

AQUARIUS MOON
BEER COCKTAIL

ENERGIES: purification, renewal, abundance, wisdom
MOON(S): in Aquarius, full moon, waning gibbous moon

The Aquarius moon can certainly bring out quirkiness, and this beer cocktail is no exception! If you're not familiar with beer cocktails, the combination of these unique elements to create something utterly different and delicious may be a bit shocking, true to Aquarius fashion. With cleansing lavender, rosemary, lemon, and sage to complement the cleansing properties of beer, this drink is perfect for purification lunar workings as well as to celebrate the abundance of the summer harvest moons.

Serves 1

2 medium fresh sage leaves
1 sprig fresh rosemary
2 dashes Lavender Bitters (see recipe in Chapter 4)
1/2 ounce Simple Syrup (see recipe in Chapter 4)
1 ounce lemon juice
1 ounce apple brandy
3–4 1/2 ounces wheat beer
1 lemon peel, for garnish

Muddle sage and rosemary with Lavender Bitters and Simple Syrup in the bottom of a cocktail shaker. Add lemon juice, brandy, and ice to fill. Shake, then double strain into a beer glass and pour beer on top. Garnish with lemon peel.

More Moon Magic

Besides its popularity for being delicious, beer actually has a history of use in baths. Replicate the rejuvenating and purifying elements of this cocktail in a beer soak by pouring some beer into your bath as you sip your drink.

LUNAR ECLIPSE HURRICANE

ENERGIES: soul shift, power, transformation

MOON(S): lunar eclipse, full moon

The lunar eclipse can be a powerful moment of transformation, elevating your spirit to the next level. It can also do this transformation in a way that causes quite a stir. Celebrate this energy with a rosy twist on the classic Hurricane cocktail. With a float of Grenadine to signify the often red color of this cosmic event, this drink is the perfect companion to the lunar eclipse in both aesthetic representation and energetic alignment. Be sure to check the corresponding solar eclipse energy to understand the effects of the current eclipse season.

Serves 1

1 ounce light rum
1 ounce dark rum
$1/2$ ounce lemon juice
$1/2$ ounce lime juice
2 ounces pulp-free orange juice
$1/2$ ounce passion fruit liqueur
$1/4$ ounce Rose, Jasmine, and Rosemary Syrup (see recipe in Chapter 4)
$1/2$ ounce Grenadine (see recipe in Chapter 4)
1 orange peel, for garnish

Place all ingredients except orange peel in a cocktail shaker and add ice to fill. Shake, knowing the moon is going to shake things up. Strain into a hurricane or red wine glass over ice. Garnish with orange peel.

More Moon Magic

A violet crystal associated with intuition, with flashes of bright orange within, iolite-sunstone is perfect for the transformative magic of the lunar eclipse. Meditate with this stone after or while consuming this beverage, connecting the duality of forces within it—as well as those around you.

MOON MAGNETISM

ENERGIES: radiance, positivity, peace, love

MOON(S): in Leo, in Libra

Aligned to the energies of both the moon and the sign of Leo, this cocktail is packed with herbal energetic potency for radiance, love, and peace of mind. Using lavender, lemon, raspberry, and orange to inspire happiness, confidence, and sensuality, this cocktail will help you to be as magnetic as the Leo moon.

Serves 1

4 fresh raspberries, divided
4 dashes rose water
$^3/_4$ ounce Rose, Jasmine, and Rosemary Syrup (see recipe in Chapter 4)
1 ounce lemon juice
3 dashes Lavender Bitters (see recipe in Chapter 4)
$^1/_2$ ounce orange liqueur
1 jigger (1$^1/_2$ ounces) spiced rum
1 lemon peel, for garnish

Add all ingredients except 1 raspberry and lemon peel to a cocktail shaker and add ice to fill. Shake, visualizing a bright lunar light glowing within and the stimulating energy of the cocktail. Double strain into a coupe glass and garnish with remaining raspberry and lemon peel. Add 1 large ice cube or sphere.

——◇—•—————— More Moon Magic ——————•—◇——

Looking to make your aura shine like the Leo moon? Here is a tea-based Lunar Glow Bath Soak you can charge up under the moon and reuse time and time again. To make it, boil 1 cup water in a small pot over high heat. Mix together 1 sprig dried rosemary, $^1/_2$ tablespoon dried or fresh lavender flowers, $^1/_8$ teaspoon ground cinnamon, 1 tablespoon dried or fresh rose petals, $^1/_2$ tablespoon dried or fresh basil, 1 thread saffron, 2 orange peels, and 1 tablespoon dried or fresh calendula flowers in a large bowl, stirring clockwise, visualizing them glowing brighter and brighter with each turn, with golden Leo moon vibrancy. Pour in water and allow to steep 5 minutes, then add to filled bath. Relax in the water as you sip your cocktail.

MOON MEDICINE

ENERGIES: cleansing, healing, ancestry

MOON(S): August moon, in Cancer, in Capricorn

The harvest moon season brings a time of celebration and culmination, but also an opportunity to reflect on familial relationships and community. Invite healing and communication in your own relationships with this ginger and rosemary cocktail. In this recipe, scotch takes center stage, its grain and barley base embodying grounding as well as rebirth and familial cycles. It's complemented by revitalizing rosemary for peace and ginger to mend all maladies.

Serves 1

2 sprigs fresh rosemary, divided
1 small slice peeled fresh ginger
$1/2$ ounce Honey Syrup (see recipe in Chapter 4)
$3/4$ ounce lemon juice
2 ounces blended scotch whisky
$1/4$ ounce triple sec
1 piece candied ginger, for garnish

Add all ingredients except 1 rosemary sprig and candied ginger to a cocktail shaker. Add ice to fill and shake, thinking about soothing honey and purifying rosemary mixing with scotch flavors, making it more palatable and heightening its unique and positive aspects. Strain into an old-fashioned glass over ice and garnish with remaining rosemary sprig and candied ginger.

More Moon Magic

Honey-brown is a deeply grounding color, and when burned as a candle, it can help connect to the earth for stability, healing, and spiritual journeying to explore familial wounds, or to neutralize and ground energy. Dress a honey-brown candle with honey, consciously thinking of the correlation between the honey in the drink and the honey on the candle. Sprinkle with ground ginger for healing and rosemary for peace. Burn within sight as you enjoy the cocktail, or in advance of serving the drink to others.

SOCIAL SELENOPHILE

ENERGIES: happiness, love, friendship

MOON(S): in Leo, in Gemini

The summer moons provide an excellent time to gather, and the Leo moon fits right into this category! This concoction, with its tantalizing blue color and flavors of orange and pineapple, is great to show off at moon parties in true Leo fashion. Not to mention its rejuvenating and fruity ingredients will encourage everyone to have a good time and socialize.

Serves 1

½ ounce lemon juice
½ ounce Simple Syrup (see recipe in Chapter 4)
¾ ounce vodka
¾ ounce light rum
½ ounce blue curaçao
2 ounces pineapple juice
1 pineapple wedge, for garnish

Pour lemon juice, Simple Syrup, vodka, and rum into a hurricane glass. Add crushed ice to fill, then top with blue curaçao and pineapple juice. Stir, then garnish with pineapple wedge.

More Moon Magic

If you're inviting some friends over for socialization, it's always a good idea to set the mood! Take a yellow candle, anoint it with some honey or oil, and dress it with dried orange and lemon peels and rose petals. Take a moment and visualize everyone having a good time. Burn the candle during the party, or beforehand.

MOONBEAM BEAUTY

ENERGIES: rejuvenation, healing, self-love, forgiveness

MOON(S): in Virgo, in Cancer, waning moons

Some moons can highlight themes of internal criticism. And luckily, the cycle of the moon offers potent opportunities to release negative self-talk and honor your inner beauty! Using lunar ingredients for love and healing, this aloe vera and rose twist on the Lemon Drop is designed to help you recognize and release the ways you have been overly critical of yourself.

Serves 1

5 fresh mint leaves, divided
$1/4$ ounce pure aloe vera gel
$1/2$ ounce lemon juice
$1/3$ ounce orange liqueur
1 jigger ($1^1/2$ ounces) vodka

Add all ingredients except 1 mint leaf to a cocktail shaker filled with ice. Shake, then strain into a coupe glass. Garnish with remaining mint leaf.

More Moon Magic

What better way to imbue some self-appreciation and soothe the soul than with self-care? Utilizing similar ingredients to this drink, you can make the following Rose and Honey Face Mask to enjoy while you call down the moon for beauty. To make it, soak 1 tablespoon dried rose petals in 2 tablespoons amber honey and $1/2$ tablespoon aloe vera gel. Muddle petals and let sit 1 hour. Mix and apply to face, leaving it on 20 minutes. Place cucumber slices on your eyes. After 20 minutes, remove cucumbers and rinse off mask with cool water.

COSMIC WISDOM APPLETINI

ENERGIES: wisdom, freedom, truth, purification

MOON(S): in Aquarius

Sip the independent and unique energies of the Aquarius moon with this Cosmic Wisdom Appletini. Sweet and sour, and tangy and endearing, personal truth and liberation have never tasted so delicious. With anise and sage for cleansing and spiritual wisdom, rose and lemon for internal optimism, and protective bourbon for grounding, this cocktail is perfect to enjoy under the Aquarius moon.

Serves 1

1/4 ounce anise liqueur
3 large fresh sage leaves
1/2 ounce Lemon Balm Ginger Syrup (see recipe in Chapter 4)
1/2 ounce lemon juice
1 ounce apple schnapps
3/4 ounce bourbon
1 sprig fresh sage, for garnish
1 horizontal slice apple with five-pointed star indentation, for garnish

1. Rinse a martini or coupe glass with anise liqueur and set aside. In a cocktail shaker, muddle 3 sage leaves in Lemon Balm Ginger Syrup. Pour in lemon juice, apple schnapps, and bourbon. Add ice to fill and shake.

2. Discard anise liqueur from rinsed glass. Double strain cocktail into rinsed glass. Garnish with sage sprig for a cleansing aroma and apple slice, displaying five-pointed star of alignment.

⟩⟩✳⟨⟨ ———— More Moon Magic ————

Naturally growing in a star shape, star anise is an herbal ally often used to connect to spiritual energy, reveal truth, enhance psychic ability, and purify. Get a star anise and gaze upon it as you sip this drink. After you have finished your beverage, meditate with the star anise in hand, and see what limitless wisdom the cosmos have for you. Keep the star anise on hand as a reminder that your moon-inspired dreams are only as limited as your beliefs.

SUPERMOON MAI TAI

ENERGIES: beauty, optimism, love
MOON(S): supermoon, full moon, in Cancer

Celebrate this supercharged lunar occasion with a fruity and refreshing Supermoon Mai Tai! A time when it is in its closest point in orbit around the earth, the supermoon can appear 14 percent larger than the typical full moon. With dark rum for grounding and positivity-inspiring ingredients like papaya and orange, this concoction is perfect to enjoy under this amplified lunar power.

Serves 1

2 large chunks peeled and seeded papaya
$1/2$ ounce orgeat
3 dashes Moon Drop Bitters (see recipe in Chapter 4)
2 dashes rose water
1 ounce white rum
$1/2$ ounce orange liqueur
$3/4$ ounce lemon juice
$1/2$ ounce dark rum
1 lemon wheel, for garnish

In a cocktail shaker, muddle papaya in orgeat. Add Moon Drop Bitters, rose water, rum, orange liqueur, and lemon juice. Add ice to fill, shake, and dump with ice into a highball glass. Float dark rum on top and garnish with lemon wheel.

More Moon Magic

Craft a Moon Oil and charge it under the supermoon to use anytime you want to draw down the moon. Simply mix together the following essential oils in a small bowl with $3/4$ ounce almond oil: 20 drops white lotus, 6 drops ginger, 4 drops rose, 9 drops lemon, and 9 drops bergamot. Pour into a bottle. Charge underneath the supermoon, and use on candles, crystals, and other ritual tools for your lunar spells throughout the year.

VIRGO MOON MOJITO

ENERGIES: cleansing/purification, the mind, positivity

MOON(S): in Virgo, full moon, waning moons

While the moon in Virgo can certainly highlight overly critical tendencies, this energy can be channeled for some moon-inspired cleansing and decluttering. Whether you are looking to organize your finances or clean your home, this concoction draws on associations of both the moon and Virgo to help illuminate and refresh your life. Imbibe the rejuvenating and mind-clearing mint, rosemary, lemon, and lime, and savor the white rum to help sweeten your disposition.

Serves 1

7 fresh mint leaves
$1/2$ sprig fresh rosemary
$3/4$ ounce Rose, Jasmine, and Rosemary Syrup (see recipe in Chapter 4)
$1/2$ ounce lemon juice
$1/2$ ounce lime juice
1 jigger ($1^1/2$ ounces) white rum
1 ounce soda water
1 sprig fresh mint

In a collins glass, muddle mint leaves, rosemary, and Rose, Jasmine, and Rosemary Syrup. Add lemon and lime juices, rum, soda water, and ice to fill. Stir and garnish with mint sprig.

More Moon Magic

Channel the magic of this mojito into a Magical Moon Spritzer to cleanse your home for better focus. Once the moon is in Virgo and you've set your intentions, make the Magical Moon Spritzer by pouring 1 ounce distilled water into a 2-ounce spray bottle. Add in $3/4$ ounce vodka, 7 drops peppermint essential oil, 7 drops lemon essential oil, 8 drops lavender essential oil, and 8 drops rose essential oil. Allow spritzer to infuse on your moon altar or under the Virgo moon overnight. Spray anytime to cleanse a space or your energy, or to help clear your mind.

HEALING HONEY MOON LEMONADE

ENERGIES: happiness, healing, peace, insight

MOON(S): in Pisces, in Virgo

With the moon in Pisces, it's the perfect time to invoke some fluid, healing energy into your own life. Using cleansing rosemary, peaceful lavender, and soothing and healing honey, this honey lemonade will help invite calm, peace, and emotional healing, so that you too can go with the flow. For a nonalcoholic version, simply omit the alcohol.

Serves 1

1 sprig fresh lavender

1 sprig fresh rosemary

$1^{1}/_{2}$ ounces Honey Syrup (see recipe in Chapter 4)

3 ounces lemon juice

1 jigger ($1^{1}/_{2}$ ounces) vodka

$1^{1}/_{2}$ ounces soda water

1 lemon wheel, for garnish

In a rocks glass, muddle lavender and rosemary into Honey Syrup. Pour in lemon juice and vodka. Add ice to fill, top with soda water, and stir. Garnish with lemon wheel.

More Moon Magic

Grab a blue candle to represent peace and water. Lightly lather it in some healing honey, then roll it in some dried lavender and rosemary so that the honey picks up the herbs. At this point, grab a peaceful and healing stone such as blue lace agate to help inspire peaceful thoughts and calm communication. Holding the stone, visualize your desired outcome, then burn the candle in sight on a fireproof dish, imagining it transforming all your woes to peace. Enjoy your drink of corresponding ingredients as the candle does its work!

HARVEST MOON MICHELADA

ENERGIES: harvest, abundance, motivation, protection

MOON(S): September moon

What better way to celebrate the bounty of harvest season moons than with a twist on the savory Bloody Mary? In this recipe, the traditional vodka is replaced with beer for a Michelada twist with more harvest flavors and associations, but feel free to use vodka, gin, or tequila.

Serves 1

1 lemon wedge, for rim
Cayenne pepper, for rim
$^1/_8$ teaspoon salt, for rim
$^1/_4$ ounce lemon juice
2 ounces tomato juice
2 ounces tomato sauce
3 dashes Worcestershire sauce
3 dashes hot sauce
$^1/_8$ teaspoon celery salt
$^1/_8$ teaspoon horseradish
$^1/_8$ teaspoon ground black pepper
2 ounces Mexican beer
1 lemon wheel, for garnish
1 stalk celery, for garnish
3 green olives, for garnish

1. Wet the rim of a collins glass with lemon wedge, then twist in a shallow dish of cayenne pepper and salt. Set aside.

2. Add remaining ingredients except beer and garnishes to a cocktail shaker. Add ice to fill and shake. Add beer and roll drink from one end of shaker to the other.

3. Dump drink with ice into rimmed glass. Garnish with lemon wheel, celery stalk, and skewered olives.

More Moon Magic

A stone of prosperity, green aventurine invites new opportunities and healing, and can also help remove the negative energy of others from your heart center. To utilize this stone, hold or keep it nearby while visualizing all the abundance you desire coming your way with each sip of the cocktail. Afterwards, keep the stone in your wallet or pocket, or on altar to continue to invite such energies in.

PISCES MOON PEACE POTION

ENERGIES: purification, peace, the mind

MOON(S): in Pisces, in Virgo, waning moons

The moon in Pisces can be a potent time to resolve differences and discuss feelings, or to instill peace within your own soul. Craft this smooth, soothing, and lightly spiced cocktail to enjoy with someone you wish to "break bread with," or drink while inviting more peace into your life under the Pisces moon.

Serves 1

1 sprig fresh rosemary
$1/8$ teaspoon ground nutmeg
$1/2$ ounce Vanilla Vodka (see recipe in Chapter 4)
2 dashes Lavender Bitters (see recipe in Chapter 4)
$1/2$ ounce lemon juice
1 ounce gin
$1/2$ ounce Violet Liqueur (see recipe in Chapter 4)
1 egg white
1 small stemmed lavender flower, for garnish

Add all ingredients except lavender flower to cocktail shaker. Shake without ice. Add ice to fill and shake again. Strain into a coupe glass and garnish with lavender flower.

More Moon Magic

Use the purifying magic of rosemary beyond this cocktail by burning dried rosemary around your home like an incense as you drink your libation, or by creating a full herb bundle with lavender and rosemary together to burn whenever you need more peace.

MULLED MOON WINE

ENERGIES: abundance, gratitude, healing, love

MOON(S): waning gibbous moon, in Virgo, in Cancer, in Taurus

Share the abundance of the moon with this white mulled wine. Following the potent full moon, the waning gibbous moon is a great time to reflect on gratitude and lunar abundance. Packed with associations for the gibbous moon phase, this spiced, soothing, and unexpected beverage is perfect for sharing with others during a breezy night under the stars.

Serves 4

6 green cardamom pods
1 cinnamon stick
1 (750 ml) bottle Riesling
4 ounces apple juice
2 ounces Lunar Limoncello (see recipe in Chapter 4)
2 ounces brandy
6 tablespoons amber honey
Peel of 1 orange
4 lemon peels
2 sprigs fresh rosemary
1/2 cup cubed peeled pear
1/8 teaspoon ground nutmeg
4 lemon slices, for garnish

1. Heat cardamom pods and cinnamon stick in a small pot over medium heat until fragrant, about 4 minutes. Pour in Riesling, apple juice, Lunar Limoncello, brandy, and honey. Stir in orange and lemon peels, rosemary, pear, and nutmeg and bring to a boil.

2. Once boiling, let simmer over medium-low heat 5 minutes, then strain into four mugs. Garnish each with a lemon slice.

———◇—•—————— More Moon Magic ——————•—◇———

On a piece of stationery, take some time to thank the moon for its abundance, either all that has manifested or all that will. Enjoy your beverage under the moon as you write, and then burn the paper if desired. If sharing this drink with others, take a moment to write them a note with a compliment or reason why you are thankful for them. Gift the note to them with some of the drink.

ASTROLOGICAL REFERENCE LIST

The following guide matches the different edible elements, crystals, and cocktails in this book to the twelve astrological seasons. Note that there are crystals listed here that are not mentioned in Parts 1 or 2. With an endless array of minerals out there, and each one having many different energies associated with it, it would take an entire book to cover them all in detail! Parts 1 and 2 look at popular crystals connected to the signs, but when aligning to a certain astrological sign, any of the crystals in this list can be substituted for those previously discussed.

ARIES MOON

- **Drink(s):** Aries Moon Mule, New Moon Beginnings Sake, Astral Motivator, Moon Mezcalita, Summer Moon Margarita, Starbound Cherry Cosmo
- **Crystals:** bloodstone, blue lace agate, carnelian, chrysoprase, citrine, fire opal, green aventurine, hawk's-eye, magnesite, pyrite, red jasper, rhodonite, sunstone
- **Edible Elements:** allspice, blackberry, cherry, cinnamon, clove, ginger, olive, pepper, poppy seed, rhubarb, rosemary

TAURUS MOON

- **Drink(s):** Cosmic Embrace, Moon Matcha, Taurus Moon Stability Sour, Wise Moon Amaretto Sour, Taurus Moon Money-Maker, Cosmic Centering Spritzer, Lunar Love Spell Sangria, Mulled Moon Wine, Maple Moon, March Moon Milk, Cacao Crescent, Cancer Moon Jasmine & Rose, Pink Moon Potion

- **Crystals:** carnelian, emerald, green calcite, green kyanite, kunzite, lepidolite, malachite, mookaite, obsidian, peridot, prehnite, rhodonite, rutilated quartz, tree agate
- **Edible Elements:** apple, apricot, banana, barley (beer), blackberry, cardamom, cherry, hibiscus, oat, passion fruit, peach, pear, raspberry, rhubarb, rose, rye, sage, thyme, vanilla, violet

GEMINI MOON

- **Drink(s):** The Twins' Creativity Potion, Gemini Moon Mint Julep, Star Slinger, Lunar State of Mind, Social Selenophile, Wise Moon Amaretto Sour, Starbound Cherry Cosmo, March Moon Milk
- **Crystals:** amazonite, hawk's-eye
- **Edible Elements:** almond, bergamot, celery, hazel, lavender, mint, parsley, pear, peppermint, pomegranate, rosemary, walnut

CANCER MOON

- **Drink(s):** Celestial Love Elixir, Cancer Moon Jasmine & Rose, Moon Mezcalita, Lunar Love Spell Sangria, Moon Blessing, Summer Moon Margarita, Moon Medicine, Moonbeam Beauty, Supermoon Mai Tai, October Moon Reviver, Lunar Alchemy, Maple Moon
- **Crystals:** carnelian, chrysocolla, citrine, jade, moonstone, morganite, opal, petalite, pink chalcedony, rose quartz, sodalite
- **Edible Elements:** aloe vera, apple, coconut, cucumber, jasmine, lemon, lemon balm, maple, oak, papaya, poppy, pumpkin, rose, violet, watermelon, wormwood

LEO MOON

- **Drink(s):** Moonlit Lion, Lion's Moon Martini, Lush Luna, Lunar Focus, Strawberry Moon Soother, Moon Blessing, Moon Magnetism, Social Selenophile, Solar Eclipse Sour, Star Slinger, Archer's Moon Bahama Mamma, Cacao Crescent

- **Crystals:** amazonite, amber, carnelian, chrysocolla, citrine, garnet, kunzite, larimar, morganite, onyx, peridot, rhodochrosite, rose quartz, sardonyx, sunstone, tigereye, topaz, yellow calcite
- **Edible Elements:** anise, cacao, cinnamon, clove, coffee, grapefruit, honey, juniper, lavender, nutmeg, oak, olive, orange, pineapple, raspberry, rosemary, saffron, walnut

VIRGO MOON

- **Drink(s):** Gemini Moon Mint Julep, Wise Moon Amaretto Sour, Celestial Transformation Potion, Lunar Focus, Moonbeam Beauty, Virgo Moon Mojito, Healing Honey Moon Lemonade, Mulled Moon Wine, Pisces Moon Peace Potion, Lunar State of Mind
- **Crystals:** amazonite, amethyst, azurite, blue topaz, carnelian, citrine, eudialyte, fluorite, fuchsite, golden apatite, golden tigereye, green aventurine, hawk's-eye, kunzite, kyanite, peridot, sapphire, smoky quartz, staurolite
- **Edible Elements:** aloe vera, bergamot, lavender, maple, nutmeg, oak, peppermint, rosemary, violet, walnut

LIBRA MOON

- **Drink(s):** Cosmic Embrace, Moon Matcha, Maple Moon, Passionate Moon Martini, Taurus Moon Stability Sour, Winter Moon Old-Fashioned, Celestial Love Elixir, Pisces Moon Chai Latte, Lush Luna, Libra Love under the Full Moon, Lunar Love Spell Sangria, Summer Moon Margarita
- **Crystals:** amethyst, ametrine, aquamarine, bloodstone, blue topaz, celestite, chrysoprase, emerald, iolite, jade, kunzite, lapis lazuli, larimar, lepidolite, malachite, mangano calcite, opal, rhodochrosite, rose quartz, sardonyx, smoky quartz, sugilite, turquoise, watermelon tourmaline
- **Edible Elements:** aloe vera, apple, apricot, cherry, maple, oat, passion fruit, peach, raspberry, rose, rye, spearmint, strawberry, thyme, vanilla, violet, wheat (beer)

SCORPIO MOON

- **Drink(s):** Aries Moon Mule, Passionate Moon Martini, The Moonlit Psychic, Lunar Alchemy, Scorpio Moon Enchantment, Lunar Love Spell Sangria, October Moon Reviver, Gemini Moon Mint Julep
- **Crystals:** aquamarine, bloodstone, carnelian, charoite, citrine, garnet, hawk's-eye, labradorite, malachite, obsidian, red jasper, rhodochrosite, rhodonite, smoky quartz, turquoise
- **Edible Elements:** allspice, basil, blackberry, clove, ginger, peppermint, pomegranate, saffron, vanilla, violet

SAGITTARIUS MOON

- **Drink(s):** Lunar Luck Tea, The Golden Moon, The Archer's Moon Bahama Mama, Sagittarius Moon Fizz, Lion's Moon Martini, The Golden Moon, Star Slinger, Gemini Moon Mint Julep
- **Crystals:** amber, amethyst, apophyllite, azurite, blue lace agate, cerussite, emerald, garnet, Herkimer diamond, iolite, labradorite, lapis lazuli, lepidolite, moss agate, peach moonstone, peridot, rhodonite, rhyolite, ruby, sodalite, star sapphire, topaz, turquoise, wulfenite
- **Edible Elements:** anise, clove, coffee, elder, ginger, maple, nutmeg, oak, rose, rosemary, sage

CAPRICORN MOON

- **Drink(s):** Stormy Dark Moon, The Golden Moon, Moon and Sand, Winter Moon Old-Fashioned, Moon over the Sea Breeze, Lunar Luxury, Moon Medicine, Pink Moon Potion
- **Crystals:** amethyst, bloodstone, blue lace agate, clear calcite, clear quartz, fluorite, galena, garnet, magnesite, malachite, moonstone, obsidian, onyx, quartz in chlorite, ruby, serpentine, star sapphire
- **Edible Elements:** barley (beer and scotch), beet, cinnamon, corn, cranberry, elder, jasmine, poppy, thyme, vinegar

AQUARIUS MOON

- **Drink(s):** Starbound Cherry Cosmo, Wise Moon Amaretto Sour, New Moon Beginnings Sake, Aquarius Moon Beer Cocktail, Cosmic Wisdom Appletini
- **Crystals:** amber, amethyst, angelite, aquamarine, blue sapphire, clear quartz, fluorite, garnet, Herkimer diamond, rhodonite, selenite, turquoise, vanadinite
- **Edible Elements:** almond, anise, apple, cherry, hazelnut, lavender, olive, peppermint, rosemary, sage, violet

PISCES MOON

- **Drink(s):** Cosmic Embrace, Lunar Alchemy, Pisces Moon Chai Latte, Dream-Time Moon Milk, Healing Honey Moon Lemonade, Pisces Moon Peace Potion, Lunar May Milk Tea Punch, Blue Moon Luck Potion
- **Crystals:** amethyst, angelite, black tourmaline, blue lace agate, celestite, danburite, fluorite, fuchsite, jade, kunzite, lapis lazuli, moonstone, rhodochrosite, ruby in zoisite, selenite, staurolite, sugilite, turquoise
- **Edible Elements:** aloe vera, anise, blueberry, clove, jasmine, maple, nutmeg, poppy, sage

EDIBLE ELEMENT ASSOCIATIONS

The following is a guide to the associations of each magical ingredient used in this book. Refer to this list anytime you wish to create a cocktail recipe with specific energies. You can also use these associations to make other spells, or work them into a ritual or meditation.

- **Agave (Mars, fire):** love, lust, rebirth
- **Allspice (Mars, Jupiter, earth, fire):** attraction, creativity, healing, luck, money
- **Aloe vera (Jupiter, Venus, moon, water):** healing, luck, protection
- **Anise (Jupiter, air):** clarity, protection, psychic abilities, purification, spirit, youth
- **Apple (Venus, air, water):** abundance, fertility, healing, longevity, love, magic, spirituality, wisdom
- **Apricot (Venus, water):** attraction, love
- **Banana (Mars, Venus, air, water):** abundance, creativity, fertility, love, money, prosperity, spirituality
- **Basil (Mars, Pluto, Venus, fire):** love, clarity, decision-making, divination, protection, purification
- **Bay leaf (sun, fire, air):** healing, protection, psychic abilities, purification, strength, success, wisdom
- **Beet (Saturn, earth):** beauty, longevity, love
- **Bergamot (Mercury, moon, Venus, air):** balance, calm, clarity, joy, money
- **Blackberry (moon, Venus, water):** fairies, grounding, healing, luck, lust, money, protection
- **Black Peppercorn (Mars, fire):** protection, purification
- **Blueberry (moon, water):** peace, protection
- **Butterfly pea flower (Venus, earth, water):** abundance, happiness, love, money, spirituality, transformation

- Cacao (Mars, fire): abundance, love, mood, prosperity
- Cardamom (Venus, water): love, lust, peace
- Celery (Mercury, fire): focus, health, lust, mind, peace, psychic abilities
- Cherry (Mercury, Venus, water, fire): attraction, happiness, love, luck
- Cinnamon (sun, fire): attraction, healing, love, lust, manifestation, power, protection, psychic abilities, spirituality, success
- Clove (Jupiter, fire): creativity, love, money, protection, purification, spirituality
- Coconut (moon, water): protection, psychic ability, purification, spirituality
- Coffee (Mars, fire): cleansing, divination, energy, mind
- Cranberry (Mars, water): abundance, action, passion, protection
- Cucumber (moon, water): beauty, healing, peace, youth
- Dill (Mercury, air, fire): abundance, health, home, love, lust, mind, money, protection, sleep (mid to late summer)
- Egg (birth of all planets and elements): creation, grounding, protection, purification, spirituality
- Elder (Venus, Mercury, air, fire, earth, water): healing, luck, prosperity, protection, purification, sleep
- Ginger (Mars, fire): love, money, power, success
- Grape (moon, water): abundance, dreams, fertility, money, spirituality
- Grapefruit (moon, water): mood, purification
- Hazelnut (sun, Mercury, air): communication, creativity, magic, protection, psychic ability, wisdom
- Hibiscus (Venus, water): love, lust
- Honey (sun, air): happiness, health, love, purification, sex, spirituality, wisdom
- Jasmine (Mercury, moon, air, earth, water): abundance, clarity, communication, creativity, dreams, fears, ideas, intuition, love, luck, money, peace, protection, psychic abilities, spirituality
- Lavender (Mercury, air): communication, fairies, fidelity, happiness, harmony, longevity, love, lust, peace, purification, sleep
- Lemon (moon, water): creativity, fidelity, friendship, happiness, joy, longevity, love, purification
- Lemon balm (moon, water): healing, love, peace, success
- Lime (sun, fire): healing, hex-breaking, love, purification
- Maple (Jupiter, air, earth): longevity, love, money

- **Melon (moon, water):** abundance, healing, love, purification
- **Milk (moon, water):** goddess worship, love, spirituality
- **Mint (Peppermint: Mercury; Spearmint: Venus):** abundance, cleansing, love, mind, peace, psychic abilities
- **Nutmeg (Jupiter, moon, fire):** fidelity, health, luck, money, mood boosting, psychic abilities
- **Oak (sun, Jupiter, air, earth, fire):** fertility, healing, health, luck, protection, strength, wisdom
- **Oat (Venus, earth):** grounding, healing, money, prosperity
- **Olive (sun, fire, air):** fertility, healing, luck, lust, peace, potency, protection, spirituality
- **Orange (sun, fire):** attraction, creativity, happiness, love, luck, optimism, prosperity, purification
- **Papaya (moon, water):** beauty, love, lust, youth
- **Passion Fruit (moon, water):** love, passion, peace
- **Peach (Venus, water):** fertility, happiness, health, love, purification, wisdom
- **Pear (Venus, moon, water):** longevity, love, lust, money
- **Pineapple (sun, fire):** creativity, happiness, healing, love, money, protection
- **Pomegranate (Mercury, fire):** abundance, creativity, fertility, luck, money, protection, wishes
- **Poppy (moon, water):** creativity, fertility, love, money, peace, sleep
- **Pumpkin (moon, earth):** abundance, divination, goddess worship, healing, money
- **Raspberry (Venus, water):** happiness, love
- **Rhubarb (Venus, earth):** fidelity, love, protection
- **Rice (sun, air):** fertility, happiness, luck, prosperity, protection, purification
- **Rose (Venus, water):** divination, healing, love, luck, protection, psychic abilities
- **Rosemary (sun, Mercury, moon, fire):** fairies, fidelity, healing, love, lust, mental powers, protection, purification, sleep, youth
- **Rye (Venus, earth):** abundance, ancestors, fidelity, love
- **Saffron (sun, fire):** happiness, healing, love, psychic abilities, strength
- **Sage (Jupiter, Mercury, earth, air):** cleansing, focus, healing, health, longevity, psychic abilities, purification, spirituality, wisdom
- **Salt (Earth, earth):** grounding, protection, purification
- **Strawberry (Venus, water):** happiness, harmony, love, luck
- **Sugarcane (Venus, water):** attraction, love, lust

- **Thyme (Venus, water):** courage, healing, love, peace, psychic abilities, purification, sleep
- **Tomato (Venus, water):** health, love, money, prosperity, protection
- **Turmeric (Mercury, air):** creativity, mood, purification
- **Vanilla (Venus, water):** energy, love, lust, mental powers, mind, peace, sexuality
- **Vinegar (Saturn, fire):** protection, purification
- **Violet (Venus, water, air):** dreams, fairies, fortune, happiness, hope, love, luck, magic, peace, psychic abilities, wishes
- **Walnut (sun, fire):** healing, mind, protection, strength, wishes
- **Watermelon (moon, water):** fertility, healing
- **Wheat (Venus, earth):** abundance, fertility, money, prosperity
- **Wormwood (moon, Mars, fire):** calling spirits, healing, love, protection, psychic powers, travel

BIBLIOGRAPHY

Bobrow, Warren. *Bitters & Shrub Syrup Cocktails: Restorative Vintage Cocktails, Mocktails & Elixirs.* Beverly, MA: Fair Winds Press, 2015.

Boland, Yasmin. *Moonology: Working with the Magic of Lunar Cycles.* Carlsbad, CA: Hay House, 2016.

Cartwright, Mark. "Soma." World History Encyclopedia. 12 May 2021, www.worldhistory.org/Soma.

Cunningham, Scott. *Cunningham's Encyclopedia of Magical Herbs.* Woodbury, MN: Llewellyn Publications, 1985.

Cunningham, Scott. *Cunningham's Encyclopedia of Wicca in the Kitchen.* Woodbury, MN: Llewellyn Publications, 1990.

de la Forêt, Rosalee. *Alchemy of Herbs: Transform Everyday Ingredients Into Foods and Remedies That Heal.* Carlsbad, CA: Hay House, Inc., 2017.

Diac, Juliet. *Plant Witchery: Discover the Sacred Language, Wisdom, and Magic of 200 Plants.* Carlsbad, CA: Hay House, 2020.

Faragher, Aliza Kelly. *The Mixology of Astrology: Cosmic Cocktail Recipes for Every Sign.* Avon, MA: Adams Media, 2018.

Forrest, Steven. *The Book of the Moon: Discovering Astrology's Lost Dimension.* Borrego Springs, CA: Seven Paws Press, Inc, 2010.

Gately, Iain. *Drink: A Cultural History of Alcohol.* New York, NY: Gothman Books, 2008.

Gottesdiener, Sarah Faith. *The Moon Book: Lunar Magic to Change Your Life.* New York, NY: St. Martin's Essentials, 2020.

Hadas, Julia. *WitchCraft Cocktails: 70 Seasonal Drinks Infused with Magic & Ritual.* Avon, MA: Adams Media, 2020

Hall, Judy. *The Crystal Zodiac: Use Birthstones to Enhance Your Life.* New York, NY: Godsfield Press, 2017.

Herkes, Michael. *The Complete Book of Moon Spells: Rituals, Practices, and Potions for Abundance*. Emeryville, CA: Rockridge Press, 2020.

Kynes, Sandra. *Llewellyn's Complete Book of Correspondences: A Comprehensive & Cross-Referenced Resource for Pagans & Wiccans*. Woodbury, MN: Llewellyn Publications, 2013.

Kynes, Sandra. *Plant Magic: A Year of Green Wisdom for Pagans & Wiccans*. Woodbury, MN: Llewellyn Publications, 2017.

Lauro, Livio. *USBG Master Accreditation Beverage & Bartending Compendium*. United States Bartenders Guild, 2017.

McCarthy, Juliana. *The Stars Within You: A Modern Guide to Astrology*. Boulder, CO: Roost Books, 2018.

Morrison, Dorothy. *Everyday Moon Magic: Spells & Rituals for Abundant Living*. Woodbury, MN: Llewellyn Publications, 2004.

Simmons, Robert, and Naisha Ahsian. *The Book of Stones: Who They Are and What They Teach*. Berkeley, CA: Heaven & Earth Publishing, 2015.

Stewart, Amy. *The Drunken Botanist: The Plants That Create the World's Great Drinks*. Chapel Hill, NC: Algonquin Books, 2013.

US/METRIC CONVERSION CHART

VOLUME CONVERSIONS

US Volume Measure	Metric Equivalent
⅛ teaspoon	0.5 milliliter
¼ teaspoon	1 milliliter
½ teaspoon	2 milliliters
1 teaspoon	5 milliliters
½ tablespoon	7 milliliters
1 tablespoon (3 teaspoons)	15 milliliters
2 tablespoons (1 fluid ounce)	30 milliliters
¼ cup (4 tablespoons)	60 milliliters
⅓ cup	90 milliliters
½ cup (4 fluid ounces)	125 milliliters
⅔ cup	160 milliliters
¾ cup (6 fluid ounces)	180 milliliters
1 cup (16 tablespoons)	250 milliliters
1 pint (2 cups)	500 milliliters
1 quart (4 cups)	1 liter (about)

WEIGHT CONVERSIONS

US Weight Measure	Metric Equivalent
½ ounce	15 grams
1 ounce	30 grams
2 ounces	60 grams
3 ounces	85 grams
¼ pound (4 ounces)	115 grams
½ pound (8 ounces)	225 grams
¾ pound (12 ounces)	340 grams
1 pound (16 ounces)	454 grams

INDEX

Note: Page numbers in **bold** indicate recipe category summaries in Contents section.
Page numbers in *italics* indicate recipes.

W

ABOUT
THE AUTHOR

JULIA HALINA HADAS is a longtime practicing witch, energy worker, and avid craft cocktail fanatic and bartender. Having worked at a distillery and as a craft cocktail bartender in the San Francisco Bay area, she combined her love of the craft cocktail movement with her spiritual practice. You can learn more at her blog, WitchCraftCocktails.com, or at JuliaHalinaHadas.com.